Scott, Foresman Reading

Golden
Secrets

Program Authors

Ira E. Aaron
Dauris Jackson
Carole Riggs
Richard G. Smith
Robert J. Tierney

Book Authors

Ira E. Aaron
Sylvia Carter

Instructional Consultants

John Manning
Dolores Perez

Scott, Foresman and Company
Editorial Offices: Glenview, Illinois

Regional Offices: Palo Alto, California
Tucker, Georgia • Glenview, Illinois
Oakland, New Jersey • Dallas, Texas

ACKNOWLEDGMENTS

"The Great Hamster Hunt" is abridged and adapted from THE GREAT HAMSTER HUNT, text copyright © 1969 by Lenore Blegvad. Reprinted by permission of Harcourt Brace Jovanovich, Inc. Published in Great Britian for the British Commonwealth by World's Work Ltd. and used with their permission.

"Before She Went Away" is reprinted by permission of G. P. Putnam's Sons from IS ANYBODY HUNGRY? by Dorothy Aldis. Copyright © 1964 by Dorothy Aldis.

"Why Wasn't I Asked to the Party?" from "Why Wasn't I Asked to the Party?" by Elizabeth Starr Hill from the September 1975 issue of *Cricket* Magazine. Used by permission of the author.

"Anya's Adventure" is adapted by permission of G. P. Putnam's Sons from ANTS DON'T GET SUNDAY OFF by Penny Pollock. Copyright © 1978 by Penny Pollock.

"Weather Wisdom" is reprinted by permission of Elsevier/Nelson Books from the book NATURE'S WEATHER FORECASTERS. Copyright © 1978 by Helen R. Sattler.

"Engine Number Seven" adapted from ENGINE NUMBER SEVEN by Eleanor Clymer. Copyright © 1975 by Eleanor Clymer. Reprinted by permission of Holt, Rinehart and Winston, Publishers.

"Song of the Train" from ONE AT A TIME by David McCord. Copyright 1952 by David McCord. By permission of Little, Brown & Company.

"I Have a Sister, My Sister Is Deaf" is the complete text of I HAVE A SISTER—MY SISTER IS DEAF by Jeanne Whitehouse Peterson. Text copyright © 1977 by Jeanne Whitehouse Peterson. By permission of Harper & Row, Publishers, Inc.

"If I Rode a Dinosaur" is an adaptation and abridgment of IF I RODE A DINOSAUR by Miriam Young. Copyright © 1974 by Miriam Young. By permission of Lothrop, Lee & Shepard Co. (A Division of William Morrow & Company) and Russell & Volkening, Inc. as agents for the author.

ISBN 0-673-21412-5

"Popular Inventions" by Webb Garrison is from the book WHY DIDN'T I THINK OF THAT? by Webb Garrison. © 1977 by Webb Garrison. Published by Prentice-Hall, Inc., Englewood Cliffs, New Jersey 07632 and used with their permission.

"Mr. Hare Takes Mr. Leopard for a Ride" from PLAYS FROM AFRICAN FOLKTALES by Carol Korty. Copyright © 1969, 1975 Carol Korty. Used by permission of Charles Scribner's Sons and Alice Bach. Requests for performance rights should be directed to the author in care of Charles Scribner's Sons.

"The Rabbit and the Fox" by Clive Sansom is from THE GOLDEN UNICORN by Clive Sansom, published by Methuen & Co. Ltd. Used by permission of David Higham Associates Limited.

Photograph of Benjamin Banneker: Used by permission of Schomberg Center for Research in Black Culture, The New York Public Library, Astor, Lenox and Tilden Foundations.

Map of Washington, D.C. in 1792: Used by permission of Map Division, The New York Public Library, Astor, Lenox and Tilden Foundations.

"The Shoeshine Chair" is an adaptation of Chapter 9, "The Shoeshine Chair," text only, from ANGIE by Janice May Udry. Text copyright © 1971 by Janice May Udry. By permission of Harper & Row, Publishers, Inc.

"Yagua Days" is adapted from YAGUA DAYS by Cruz Martel. Copyright © 1976 by Cruz Martel. Reprinted by permission of The Dial Press.

"Raining" from STORIES TO BEGIN ON by Rhoda W. Bacmeister. Copyright 1940 by E. P. Dutton & Co., Inc. Renewal ©, 1968 by Rhoda W. Bacmeister. Reprinted by permission of the publisher.

"The Baobab Automobile" is adapted from "The Baobab Automobile" by Jacqueline Held from the March 1975 issue of *Cricket* Magazine. Reprinted by permission of the author.

Photo of baobab tree: Used by permission of *Photo Researchers, Inc.*

"The Pumpkin Tree" is adapted from "The Pumpkin Tree" by Ryerson Johnson from the March 1974 issue of *Cricket* Magazine. Reprinted by permission of the author.

"Why Cowboys Sing, in Texas" is an excerpt from WHY COWBOYS SING, IN TEXAS by Le Grand (Henderson). Copyright © 1950 by Le Grand Henderson. Reprinted by permission of McIntosh and Otis, Inc.

(Acknowledgments continued on page 380)

CONTENTS

SECTION ONE

The Great Hamster Hunt

by Lenore Blegvad

Nicholas wanted a hamster. Mother and Father said no to that.

"But Tony has a hamster," Nicholas said.

"Nicholas, you know your mother and I aren't too crazy about little furry creatures," Father remarked.

8

One day Tony came to the door.

"We're going away for a week," he said to Nicholas's mother. "Do you think Nicholas would take care of my hamster for me?"

Jumping up from his chair, Nicholas shouted, "The answer is yes!"

So Tony's hamster came to stay with Nicholas for a week. Its name was Harvey. It lived in a shiny cage with wire on top and a sliding wall of glass in front. There was also a wheel that went around and around when Harvey ran inside it.

Before Tony left, he told Nicholas how to take care of Harvey.

"Can I take him out of his cage?" Nicholas asked as Tony was leaving.

"Sure," Tony said. "But watch out he doesn't disappear. So long." Then, halfway across the garden, he called, "Hey, I forgot to tell you. Hamsters are nocturnal, in case you didn't know. So long."

"What's that mean?" Nicholas called back. But Tony had already gone.

All that week Nicholas took good care of Harvey. He fed him and played with him and cleaned his cage carefully. But he always remembered that Harvey was Tony's hamster. He would hold Harvey in his hand, and he would whisper, "Oh, I wish I had a hamster just like you!"

All too soon the week was up. Tony would be coming home the next evening. After supper Nicholas decided to clean Harvey's cage for the last time. He took it down to the kitchen. First he put Harvey in a large carton. Then, very carefully, he slid out the glass panel from the cage, and very carefully he started to put the glass on the table, but all of a sudden . . .

CRASH!

The glass slipped from his hands and broke into a million pieces all over the kitchen floor!

Nicholas's father helped to sweep them up.
Then his father found a piece of cardboard,
cut it to the right size, and slid it into the
place where the glass had been. It worked well.

When they had finished, it was time for
Nicholas to go to bed. He was very sad because
it was Harvey's last night in his house.
Nicholas put him in the cage and looked at him
through the wires on top.

"Good night, Harvey," he whispered. "We sure
had a good time, didn't we?" Then he soon fell
asleep to the sound of the squeaking exercise
wheel.

When morning came, Nicholas looked in through
the top of the cage to say good morning, but . . .
would you believe it? The cage was empty!

"Oh, no!" Mother said when she heard.

"Oh, no!" Father said when he went to see.
"He's chewed a hole through the cardboard."

So they began to look—right then, before breakfast.

They looked under Nicholas's bed. They looked in his dresser drawers. They looked in his closet and in all the boxes in the closet and in all the pockets of all the clothes in the closet. They looked in the toy box and behind the curtains and under Nicholas's pillow.

When they had not found a trace of Harvey, Father said, "He could be anywhere, you know."

"And we'll never find him before Tony comes back," Nicholas said, and looked as though he might cry.

"What are we going to do?" Mother asked.

All at once, Father seemed to have the answer.

"We must go on a hunt for him," he said firmly. "As if he were a lion, or an elephant. We must bring him back alive! And to do that, we must trap him." He jumped up. "First," he continued, "I'll need lots of plastic wastebaskets." He then dressed quickly and rushed out of the house.

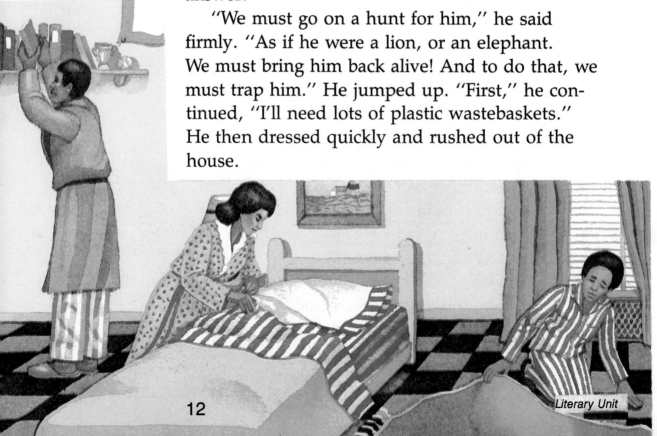

While he was gone, Nicholas and his mother continued to look for Harvey. They were still looking when Father came back with eight plastic wastebaskets. He also brought a new piece of glass for Harvey's cage.

Then he put a small pile of books in the middle of each room in the house and leaned a wastebasket against each pile.

"Now," he said, "I need blocks, long wooden blocks, Nicholas. And towels," he said to Mother. "Plenty of towels. And don't forget the lettuce."

So Father took the blocks and the towels and the lettuce and he made . . . hamster traps!

"Now, all we have to do is to wait for Harvey to eat his way up the ramp and fall into one of the wastebaskets," Father explained. "The plastic is too slippery for him to climb out." And he started to read his morning paper.

Mother looked at Nicholas.

"Do you think . . . ?" Nicholas began.

"Not really," Mother said, and picked up her purse. "We'd better take a little shopping trip, just in case."

Mother took Nicholas downtown. They tried
many pet stores until quite late in the afternoon. But when they got to the last pet shop,
they were relieved to see a hamster that looked
very much like Harvey. It was white with pink
eyes and a pink nose.

The shopkeeper put the hamster in a little
cardboard box with air holes. Nicholas held it
carefully on his lap on the way home. He felt
much better now. At least Tony would have a
hamster that could remind him of Harvey.

14

When they got home, Nicholas put the new hamster in Harvey's cage. It ran around in Harvey's treadmill a few times. Then it curled up in a corner of the cage and went to sleep.

"I hope Tony will get to like you as much as he liked Harvey," Nicholas said to it. "Anyway, I like you. I wish you were my hamster."

"And I wish those traps had worked," Father said, looking at his wastebaskets.

"I don't know about you," Mother said, turning on the lamps in the living room, "but I'm exhausted. I am going to play myself some relaxing music." She sat down at the piano.

"A nocturne would do it," Father said, settling down to listen. Nicholas turned his head.

"A what?" he asked. Where had he heard that word before?

"A nocturne is a piece of night music, dreamy, cloudy kind of music. The word *nocturne* has to do with night."

"Then that's what Tony meant," Nicholas cried, jumping up. "And that's why Harvey sleeps all day and plays all night. All hamsters do. They're nocturnal!"

Running up the stairs to his room Nicholas shouted, "Now is the time to look for Harvey!" He tiptoed over to his bed and sat down in the dark. Everything was very quiet. Then downstairs his mother started playing the nocturne—very softly. Nicholas listened, but he was also listening for something else—for the sound of a hamster waking up to play.

Then he heard it. A rustle and a scratch.
And another rustle and another scratch! It came
from underneath his bookshelf! Nicholas turned
on his lamp just in time to see Harvey's pink
nose poking out from the tiniest crack between
the bookshelf and the wall!

Nicholas waited until Harvey had squeezed
himself out into the room, and then he swooped
down and picked him up.

"I've got him!" he called to his parents, and
ran downstairs.

"Good for you," Father said. "That's the way
to hunt hamsters!"

"I never thought I'd consider a hamster so
absolutely beautiful," said Mother, patting
Harvey.

Then Nicholas put Harvey back in his cage. The two hamsters stared at each other for a moment. Then the new hamster returned to the exercise wheel and Harvey began to eat.

Nicholas and his parents watched them, and Nicholas began to feel a strange feeling of wildest hope. He looked at his mother and father. Did he dare ask?

"Do you think . . ." he began, ". . . if I took very good care of him . . . that maybe . . . ?" His mother and father nodded, almost together.

"Yes," his father said. "You're an expert on hamsters. I don't see why you shouldn't have one of your own."

"Yes," agreed Nicholas's mother. "I rather like hamsters now."

Just then the doorbell rang. It was Tony.
He had come to fetch Harvey. He was very
surprised to see another white hamster in
Harvey's cage. Nicholas took his new hamster
out, and it ran up his arm to sit on his
shoulder.

"Hey," Tony said. "How come you got a
hamster? It's not your birthday or anything, is it?"

Nicholas shook his head. "No," he said
happily. "It was just by accident."

Tony was puzzled. "Oh" was all he said, as
if he understood. But he didn't. "Well, thanks
a lot for taking care of Harvey."

Nicholas went with him to the door. "You're welcome," he said. "See you tomorrow."

In the mirror next to the front door, Nicholas saw himself with his hamster. The hamster was sitting on Nicholas's head. It looked very happy up there, and underneath it Nicholas looked happy too.

Comprehension Check

1. Why did Nicholas take care of Tony's hamster for a week? How did he feel about taking care of Tony's hamster?
2. What did the hamster traps that Nicholas's father made look like? Why do you think they didn't work?
3. Why did Nicholas's mother take him to the pet store?
4. When did Nicholas understand the meaning of the word *nocturnal*? What does *nocturnal* mean?
5. Have you ever taken care of a pet for a friend? What did you need to know in order to take care of the pet?

BEFORE SHE WENT AWAY

by Dorothy Aldis

Miss Jones, before she went away,
Brought her hamster in his cage
For me to care for every day.

He is very plump and small.
He hardly has a tail at all—
Just a silly little stump.
But everything else he needs is there:
Ears and whiskers,
Eyes and hair.

I keep his cage clean.
Fill his tray
With lettuce,
Apples,
Sunflower seed.
I let him out and hope he'll play.
He doesn't really want to though.
He'd rather take a nap all day.

But what a scurry later on.
Night's no time for him to sleep!
So when I wake I'm not alone.
I love it having company.
I wrote Miss Jones and told her this
And guess what she wrote back to me?
"My hamster is *your* hamster now
To keep."

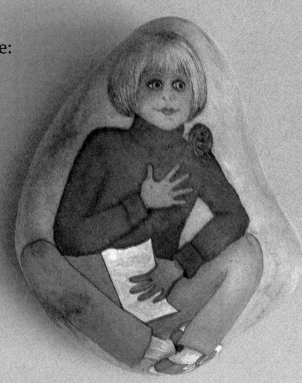

Looking for Time Clues

Sometimes it is important to know when the action in a story takes place. The author usually gives you time clues that help you understand when events in the story take place.

A time clue may be a date like 1892 or 2056. A time clue may be words like <u>three weeks</u>, <u>yesterday</u>, <u>twenty years</u>, <u>before dinner</u>, <u>in the afternoon</u>, or <u>long ago</u>.

Read the story below. Look for the time clues.

Early one morning in 1825, Josiah Jefferson got ready for his trip to town. After he ate breakfast, he hitched his horses to the wagon in front of his house. Then he climbed into the seat and called to the horses to start moving. Four hours later he arrived in town.

Answer the following questions about time clues in the story you just read.

1. In what year did the story take place?
2. At what time of day did the story take place?
3. When did Josiah hitch his horses to the wagon?
4. How long did the trip take?

Practice

Read the next story. What time clues does the author use to help you know when the events in the story happen?

The Galaxy 301 spaceship landed smoothly on planet Degar. The ship had left Taxos in the year 2190. Now, one year later, the journey was completed.

Before the giant door of the spaceship opened, everyone was silent. They hoped this planet would be safe. They had only three hours to find out if they could live on Degar.

Answer the following questions about time clues in the story about Galaxy 301.

1. In what year did the spaceship leave Taxos?
2. How long did the trip to Degar take?
3. In what year did the spaceship land on Degar?
4. How long did the people have to find out if they could live on Degar?

As you read about Jan in the next story, look for time clues that help you know when the events in the story take place.

Why Wasn't I Asked to the Party?

by Elizabeth Starr Hill

Jan walked home from school slowly. The question she was asking herself over and over again made her hurt inside.

Why wasn't I asked to the party?

When she reached her house, her younger brother Bart came to meet her, carrying a baseball and a bat. "Want to throw the ball for me?"

Jan did not really want to, but she knew he had been waiting for her. "OK."

Bart missed most of the balls but hit a few.

"Let's stop and get some milk," Jan said finally.

They raced each other to the house. The kitchen smelled spicy-warm. Their mother was just taking fresh-baked apple tarts from the oven.

"Have one each," she offered. She poured milk and sat with Jan and Bart at the kitchen table.

As they ate, Jan thought about the party again. At school, she had heard Suellen and Christine and Mary Lou talking about Vicky's invitation for Saturday afternoon. She had kept quiet, not wanting anyone to know she had not gotten one.

"Is something wrong?" Mom asked.

"No!" Jan clattered from the table and ran upstairs.

On the landing, the low window seat seemed inviting. Jan curled up on its cushions and looked out. Bart was practicing batting again. "He doesn't get discouraged," she thought. "He practices every afternoon, batting, missing, trying again. He never gets discouraged.

"Me, though . . . I gave up right away, when I wasn't asked to the party."

An idea stirred in Jan's mind. What if she could figure out a plan to get herself invited? Things might be made to work out right after all.

She remembered the puppet Aunt Lucy had given her last Christmas. It had handles and strings, and she never learned how to manage it. Now the thought of it held possibilities.

She pounded downstairs. "Mom! You know my puppet that you put away in the attic? Could we find it?"

"I don't know," said Mom, "but we can certainly look."

They climbed the ladder stairs and searched the cobwebby attic. They saw a long, familiar box. The elegant wooden lady lay inside. She wore a white wig, a ball gown, and dainty slippers.

"Oh, Mom," Jan cried. "Could you help me learn to make her dance? Right away? Tonight?"

Mom smiled. "Right after supper, if your homework's done."

Jan finished her lessons in record time, and Jan got out the puppet.

Her mother wasn't quite sure how to go at it either. "Take one set of strings in each hand, and let's see what happens," she suggested.

Jan did, but it was hard. The puppet stumbled around, her arms flopping, her head wagging oddly from side to side.

But gradually Jan began to get the hang of it. At last the puppet danced to her whistled tune, straight across the kitchen table.

"Hurray!" Mom cheered.

That night Jan lay awake a long time. She imagined Vicky's birthday cake, ice cream, and games. And she decided exactly what to do and say to make her wish come true.

Next morning at recess, she carried the puppet to the playground. Vicky was playing tag with some other kids. Jan waited until the bell rang and the game broke up. Then, nervous but determined, she went to Vicky and told her, "I've got a puppet in this box."

"Oh," Vicky said.

"Want to see it?"

"Sure," Vicky said.

"Let's meet out here for lunch then. I know how to work it."

"OK," Vicky said.

The rest of the morning, Jan worried and worried. Then she decided Vicky wouldn't meet her anyway. In the few weeks since school had started, they had hardly gotten to know each other. They had never met for lunch before, or to play after school.

But at noon, when she went to the playground, Vicky was waiting. After they had eaten their sandwiches, Jan took the puppet from its box. She whistled her tune. To her great relief, the wooden lady danced with style and grace and did not stumble once.

When she stopped, Vicky clapped her hands. "She's beautiful! And you're a good puppeteer, Jan."

Jan gulped, and then she brought out the sentence she had planned so carefully. "A puppet show is—well, it's the kind of thing that's a lot of fun at a party." She did not dare look at Vicky's face.

"I bet," Vicky said, rather distantly. The bell rang. "Race you to the room!" She ran away.

Jan stood still, crushed with disappointment. She put the puppet back in its box. She had trouble keeping her mind on her work for the rest of the afternoon.

When she got home she pitched for Bart, thinking about her problem the whole time.

Jan almost—but not quite—decided to give up.

On Friday, the day before the party, she was miserable in school. She heard Suellen say she was planning to wear her yellow dress to Vicky's. Christine and Mary Lou were going in the same car pool.

Then, after the very last class, she heard Vicky and Christine talking about Skittaloo, a new game in the stationery store. "I'm saving up for it," Vicky said. "It's expensive, though."

A last bright hope came to Jan. She blurted, "I was planning to give you Skittaloo for your birthday."

Vicky's face went stiff and wary.

Jan's voice faltered as she went on. "I— well, I guess I'll drop it at your house. In the morning."

Vicky seemed a little angry. Then in a cool, resigned tone she replied, "Bring it in the afternoon. Come to my party." She wheeled and walked away.

Jan waited to feel thrilled. Or glad, even. Or relieved, at least. Instead, she was badly mixed-up. When she imagined the party now, it did not seem wonderful anymore. The thought of it made her ashamed.

She did not know what to do. She needed help.

At home, she found her mother reading on the side porch. "Mom, I have to talk to you," she burst out.

She explained how she hadn't been asked to the party. And how she had schemed to get invited.

"Now I don't even want to go. So why did I feel so bad about not being asked in the first place?" Jan's words spilled out in a rush.

Her mother considered carefully. Then she said, "You probably thought there was something wrong

with you. Some awful reason for Vicky to leave
you out. But it wasn't that." She smiled into
Jan's eyes. "Vicky just doesn't know how special
you are."

Inside Jan the pain seemed to go away. She
started to ask, "Am I special?" But the answer
was already there, in her mother's smiling face.

Mom added gently, "It happens to everybody,
sooner or later, that you don't get asked to a
party. And it really doesn't matter much. Having
Vicky for a friend would matter more."

That night Jan sat on the window seat until
it was very dark outside. She thought over what
her mother had said.

Next morning she emptied her coin bank
and borrowed two extra dollars from Bart.
She bought Skittaloo.

She asked the lady in the stationery store
to wrap it in fancy paper with a ribbon bow.
She skipped the whole way to Vicky's house
and rang the bell.

Vicky answered the door. Jan thrust the
present at her. "It's for you, it's Skittaloo.
I can't come to the party, but—" She
caught her breath and grinned. "Happy
birthday."

Vicky looked surprised. Then delight spread over her face. She took the present, stammering her thanks.

As Jan turned to go, Vicky asked suddenly, "Can you come play tomorrow?"

Jan nodded. She skipped on home, happy, light as a bubble.

She burst into the kitchen and called out to her mother, "Mom! I just got the absolute *best* invitation I've had all week!"

Comprehension Check

1. How did Jan feel about not being invited
   to Vicky's party? Why?
2. What was Jan's first plan to get herself
   invited?
3. Why do you think Vicky didn't invite Jan
   to her party?
4. Why do you think Jan was not thrilled when
   she finally was invited?
5. Do you think Jan is the kind of person who
   gives up easily? Why do you think as you do?
6. What do you think of Jan's plans for getting
   invited to Vicky's party? Do you think Jan
   was right in trying to get invited to
   Vicky's party? Why or why not?

Skill Check

1. When was Vicky's birthday party?
2. When did Aunt Lucy give Jan the puppet?
3. At what time of day did Jan meet Vicky to show
   her the puppet?
4. On what day did Jan buy Skittaloo for Vicky?

Anya's Adventure

by Penny Pollock

Anya sat down to rest in the underground hallway. She was a small black ant. All her life she had lived in the nest under the flat gray rock. Every day she worked and worked and worked. Every night she worked and worked and worked.

Matilda, the head worker ant, came by and saw Anya sitting down.

"The queen needs workers to carry her new eggs," she said crossly.

Anya went back to work, but she was very tired. "What I need is a small holiday," she said, as she glued a mound of new eggs together and carried them to the warm nursery.

"What I need is a short trip," she said, as she pulled a baby ant from its cocoon and licked it.

"What I need is a small adventure," she said, as she stretched out the baby ant's legs. Then she sat down to rest again.

Matilda came by. "There is no time for that," she said.

"I am tired of working," Anya said. "Could I have a day off?"

Matilda just frowned.

Anya yawned, and then she washed her face. Suddenly she kicked up her six heels all at once and called out, "I want to live!" But she had forgotten that she was in the cramped hallway under the gray rock. She banged her left feeler on the dirt ceiling and bent it to one side. It seemed as if her life would never change.

Then one morning a great black cloud hung over the flat gray rock. Anya was underground, working. Rain fell from the great black cloud onto the rock and pounded down for days and days and nights and nights.

Finally the rain found the front-door opening of the nest and rushed down the hallway. Water filled every room, even the warm nursery. Anya ran for her life and so did the other ants. They tumbled on top of one another, scrambling for the doorway.

Anya was almost at the doorway when she remembered the queen.

"Stop," Anya called loudly. "We have to save the queen."

The other ants tried to push past her, but Anya would not budge. She knew her duty even if she did want a holiday. The other ants felt cross and wet and scared, but they knew Anya was right. Together they carried the queen out to high ground on top of a twig.

"And now for the baby ants," Anya said.

The hallway floor was muddy and the ants slipped and slid and struggled. Finally the baby ants were carried to safety, and some of the workers stayed to lick the baby ants dry.

Then Anya said, "We can't forget the eggs."

The rest of the ants followed Anya once more into the nest, because they could see she knew her duty. Down the damp and dangerous hallway, they went to the nursery far under the ground. Each worker picked up an egg and struggled back up the hallway. Finally the queen, the baby ants, and the eggs were above the ground.

40

The rest of the workers licked them dry, but Anya was worried. Some eggs were missing, she was sure. Anya crawled under the flat gray rock alone. The mud stuck to her feet but she sloshed slowly down, down to the nursery. There were three eggs left.

Carefully Anya squeezed the eggs tightly in her jaw and started for safety. Twice she was almost stuck in the mud. At last, tired all the way through, she reached the safe outdoors. But when she looked for the other ants, she could not see a single one.

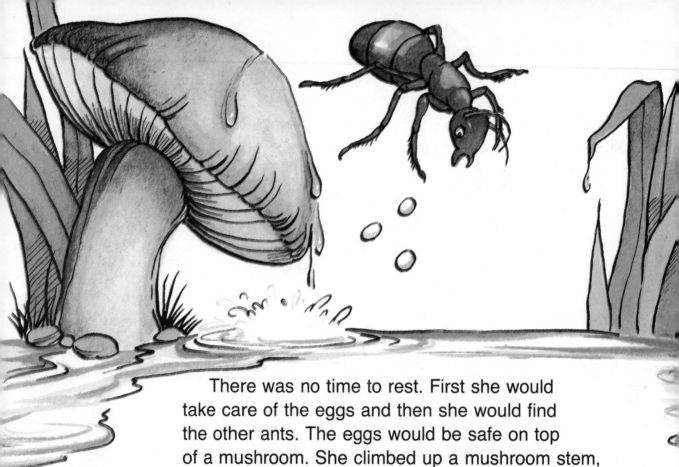

There was no time to rest. First she would
take care of the eggs and then she would find
the other ants. The eggs would be safe on top
of a mushroom. She climbed up a mushroom stem,
but lost her balance.

She slipped down the wet stem and fell on her
back in a puddle. She waved all six legs in
the air and yelled, "Help!" That made her
drop the eggs. Half-drowned, she watched as
one by one the eggs were carried away by the
rainwater. Anya got mad. "I will get them no matter
what," she said. With all the strength she had
left, she twisted and turned until she flipped
onto her feet.

She splashed to the side of the puddle and
crawled out, wet, tired, and determined. After
a giant shake to get the water out of her
joints, Anya limped after the eggs.

42

Water was everywhere. She searched for the eggs, but they were gone! Then she looked for her nest, but she could not find it either.

Anya climbed up a long dandelion stem, and she stood on top of the yellow blossom and searched for the flat gray rock. All she saw was water.

She was wet and tired and lonely. She had lost three eggs and her nest. She started to lick her front left leg for comfort when a huge raindrop hit her on the head. It knocked her off the dandelion.

She landed on an upturned oak leaf in a pool of water. The oak leaf began to turn circles in the water, and Anya felt dizzy. She crawled to the stem of the leaf and held on. She had just grabbed hold when the leaf tumbled into a ditch.

The ditch water raced on until it fell into a stream. Anya was in for a wild trip. It ended with a crash against a log, which flung her through the air. Luckily she landed on soft sand, and she stood up shakily and tried her legs. All six still worked. She tried her feelers, both of which still worked.

"All I need is a short rest," she said. "Then I must find my nest."

After a short rest, Anya raised her feelers to smell for her nest. She did smell something. Was it her nest? No, but it was a sweet smell, and Anya was as hungry as an ant with two empty stomachs can be. She waded through the grass forest toward the sweet smell. It was getting closer.

Then she saw what she had smelled. It was huge and pink, and it sparkled with wetness from the rain. Anya was so excited that she hunched down and sprang up and then landed squarely on all six feet. And every foot got stuck! She had landed on a gigantic mountain of chewed bubble gum!

44

When she tried to pull one leg free, the other five sank in deeper. She was in gum up to her knees. Anya was in trouble and she knew it. Every time she moved, she sank in deeper. She thought about her nest, and she missed all the other ants, even Matilda.

"Help!" Anya called. No one answered. She was stuck all night. It was a long, dark, lonely night. In the morning she said, "I am going to get off here no matter what." She waved her feelers in the air to find someone to help her. There was no one there. She stopped with a jerk. She had just smelled something wonderful. Home!

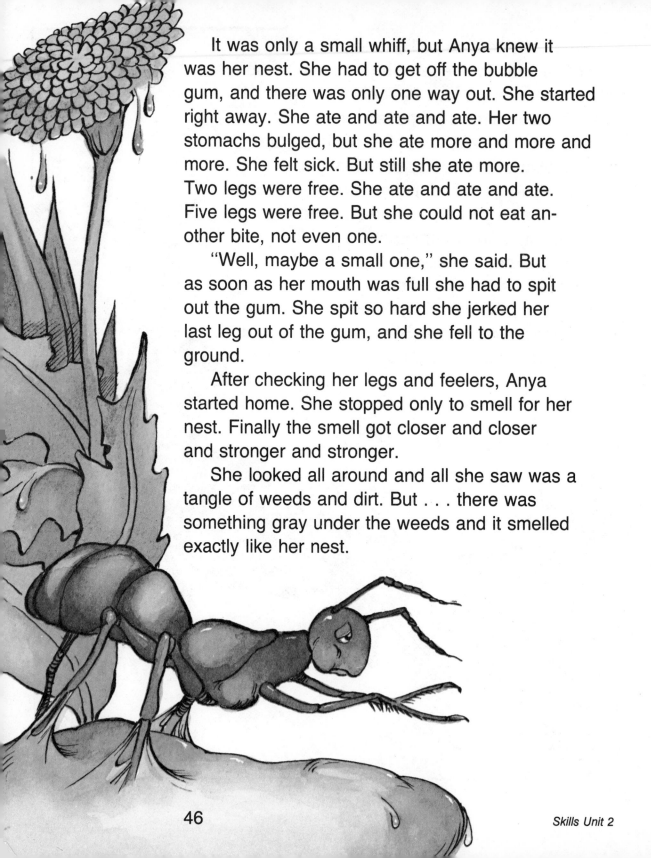

It was only a small whiff, but Anya knew it was her nest. She had to get off the bubble gum, and there was only one way out. She started right away. She ate and ate and ate. Her two stomachs bulged, but she ate more and more and more. She felt sick. But still she ate more. Two legs were free. She ate and ate and ate. Five legs were free. But she could not eat another bite, not even one.

"Well, maybe a small one," she said. But as soon as her mouth was full she had to spit out the gum. She spit so hard she jerked her last leg out of the gum, and she fell to the ground.

After checking her legs and feelers, Anya started home. She stopped only to smell for her nest. Finally the smell got closer and closer and stronger and stronger.

She looked all around and all she saw was a tangle of weeds and dirt. But . . . there was something gray under the weeds and it smelled exactly like her nest.

46

"Hello there!" she called.

The other ants smelled her and crawled out to greet her. They tapped Anya with their feelers, to say they were glad to see her. She tapped them back. Then Matilda crawled out, carrying dirt away from the caved-in doorway.

"Anya," she said. "Don't waste time. There is a lot of work to be done."

This time Anya laughed. All of a sudden work was just what she wanted to do.

Comprehension Check

1. What chores does a worker ant do?
2. What was Anya's reaction when the nest was first flooded?
3. What did Anya and the other ants do when their nest was flooded?
4. Do you think Anya is a very responsible ant? Why or why not?
5. Why was Anya happy to be working at the nest at end of the story?
6. What did you learn about ants from the story?

Skill Check

Use the Contents on page 3 of this book to answer the following questions.

1. On what page does the story "Anya's Adventure" begin?
2. Who wrote the story "The Great Hamster Hunt"?
3. On what page does the story "Engine Number Seven" begin? Who wrote the story?

Figuring Out Mystery Words

You are a great detective. You have to solve a little mystery whenever you come to a word that doesn't look familiar. The meaning of the sentence and the consonants in the mystery word are clues that help you.

Kim showed Greg how to build a m_____ airplane.

What word might make sense in the sentence? What kind of plane might Kim show Greg how to make?

The consonant m is another clue. It tells you that the mystery word begins with the sound the letter m stands for.

Look at another consonant in the mystery word.

Kim showed Greg how to build a m_____l airplane.

You may think metal is the mystery word. It makes sense, and two of the consonants match. But a detective has to study all the clues. Here is another consonant in the mystery word.

Kim showed Greg how to build a m__d__l airplane.

The mystery word isn't metal! The second consonant in metal doesn't match the second consonant in the mystery word.
There is another word that makes sense in the sentence. That word also has the same consonants as the mystery word. Do you know what the word is? The word is model.

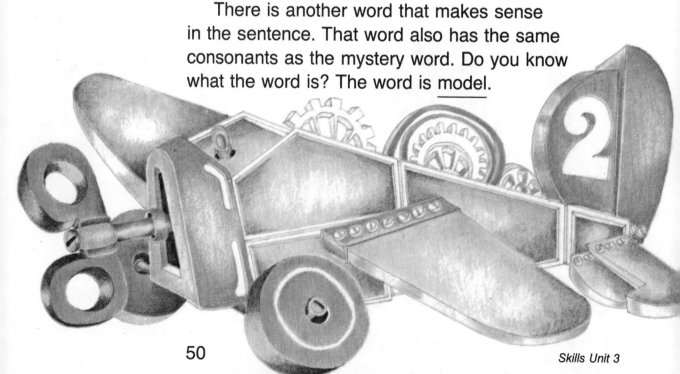

Practice

Which of the three words below each sentence makes the best sense in the blank? Use the meaning of each sentence and the consonants as clues.

1. Kim is interested in airplanes and she hopes to become a p_____ someday.
   a. peanut   b. flier   c. pilot

2. Greg is very good at making things with p_____r, wood, and string.
   a. pepper   b. hammer   c. paper

3. Greg and Kim decided to enter a kite-flying c_nt____.
   a. match   b. contest   c. center

4. Greg put all the w____d__n parts together and Kim made sure it would fly.
   a. widen   b. plastic   c. wooden

5. The kite that Greg and Kim made won a blue r_____n.
   a. robin   b. prize   c. ribbon

Use the meanings of the sentences and the consonants as clues to figure out unfamiliar words in the next story about the weather.

Weather Wisdom

by Helen Sattler

A long time ago when people lived mostly out-of-doors, they were close to nature. They noticed that plants, animals, insects, and birds could tell when bad weather was on its way sooner than people could.

Animals are born with an inner feeling or instinct to save their own lives. When they feel a storm coming, they hurry to find a safe place to stay. So the people of long ago learned to watch these signs. When the animals hurried to safe places, so did the people.

Of course, plants and animals cannot really tell when a storm is coming. They act in special ways because of changes in the air about them. The air's pressure, wetness, and temperature all make up the weather. So does the amount of wind. A change in one of these can cause a change in the way plants and animals act.

The special actions of spiders tell people when there is a lot of moisture in the air. Spiders work overtime building more and larger webs when the air is moist. The spiders seem to know that a lot of moisture in the air soaks the wings of insects and makes it harder for them to fly. So it is easier for the spiders to catch them.

However, just before a storm, the spiders take down their webs. They seem to know that a heavy rain would wash away all the bugs in the web.

Frogs and toads also give weather clues. These
animals rarely come out on dry days. They seem
to know that they will catch insects more easily
on cool and moist days. That is also why you
can hear a greater number of frogs just before
a rain.

Some people watch ants for weather clues. When ants begin to build huge mounds around their holes, be on the lookout for rain. Their work begins about two hours before a downpour. All kinds of ants will hurry to their nests and begin building dams around the ant hill. These tall mounds of dirt stop the rainwater from running into the ant hills. The ants will stay inside until the rain is over.

Bees give weather clues too. Several hours before a rain they become much busier than usual. However, just before the rain starts to fall, they return to their hives. Most of the time it will rain in about two hours. Some people say that the longer the bees work before the rain, the longer the rain will be.

Other insects can also tell us how much moisture there is in the air. Butterflies usually flit from flower to flower all day long. When they suddenly disappear and are found on the undersides of leaves, get ready for rain. They are trying to protect their wings from a hard rain.

Fireflies fly very low when there is a lot of moisture in the air. And if you hear lots of locusts singing, you can be sure that the air is dry. Locusts sing only when it is hot and dry.

58

Some people can tell what the weather is going to be like without any special instruments at all. When the air is very damp, they feel uncomfortable. It is sometimes painful for them to move. That is why these people say, "It's going to rain. I can feel it in my bones." They really can.

If you learn to read weather signs, you can tell when a storm is coming. This warning might keep you from getting your shoes ruined in the rain or having a family picnic spoiled. It will help you know what to wear so that you can even have fun in the rain.

Comprehension Check

1. What are some of the insects that act as "weather signs"?
2. What changes in the air cause the insects to behave differently?
3. How do spiders tell us about the weather?
4. What are some of the advantages of being able to read weather signs?
5. What weather signs have you seen? What did they tell you?

Skill Check

Which of the three words below each sentence makes the best sense in the blank? Use the meaning of each sentence and the consonants as clues.

1. Some people can tell what the w___t___r is going to be like without any special instruments at all.
   a. weather   b. wetter   c. fishing
2. Ants begin to build mounds around their holes when the air is m___st.
   a. most   b. moist   c. damp
3. Sp___d___rs work overtime building more and larger webs when the air is moist.
   a. caterpillars   b. spenders   c. spiders
4. Learning to read weather signs might keep you from having a family p___n___c spoiled.
   a. picnic   b. trip   c. panic

Literary Unit

Engine Number Seven

by Eleanor Clymer

Up north in the state of Maine, there was a small village named Hogus. Hogus had some white houses, a general store, a hotel, and a one-room school. It also had a train.

It was a very small train. It ran on a track only two feet wide. On the front and sides of the engine, the number seven was painted in gold.

Everybody in Hogus loved Number Seven. But especially Dot and Sam. Dot lived across the street from the train station. Mr. Hobbs, the engineer, was her grandpa. Dot's best friend was Sam Beatty. Mrs. Beatty, who ran the hotel, was his mother. Every chance they got, Dot and Sam went down to the train yard to help take care of Number Seven.

62

However, things were changing in Hogus. It was Mr. Bodger who started the changes. Besides owning the store, he was also on the town council.

One day after school, Dot and Sam saw a red truck in front of Mr. Bodger's store.

"Is that yours, Mr. Bodger?" Sam asked.

"Yes, it is," said Mr. Bodger. "Now I don't have to wait around for the train. Get in and I'll take you for a little ride."

Dot and Sam got in, and off they went. But they didn't like it. A number of people agreed with them. But others thought having your own truck was a good idea.

Then one evening Mr. Bodger called a meeting.

"Friends," said Mr. Bodger, looking very important. "I'm here to get things done. Times are changing. Now, lots of people in this town have cars or trucks. Why do we need to spend money to keep up the railroad?"

Everybody thought Mr. Bodger was right, except for Mr. Hobbs and his assistant Mr. Griggs, Dot, and Sam.

"What about Number Seven?" Dot asked.

"We might as well sell her for junk," Mr. Bodger said.

"No!" shouted Mr. Hobbs. "You'll never do that. I'll buy her myself."

And he got up and stamped out of the hall.

Dot and Sam ran after him.

"What will you do with her?" asked Dot.

"That's the trouble," said Mr. Hobbs sadly. "I don't rightly know."

A few days later Mr. Hobbs ran the little train into the shed. And there she stayed.

64

Summer came. One day, on the way to the pond with their bathing suits, Dot and Sam passed the railroad yard.

Dot said, "Too bad Number Seven's not running. It'd be a good day for a train ride."

Sam said, "Let's go inside and see her."

There in the shed stood Number Seven, all alone. Dot climbed up into the cab. Spider webs got into her hair. A bird flew out from somewhere. Then Dot and Sam heard voices. Mr. Bodger was talking to Mr. Hobbs.

"Times are changing," he said. "You can't keep this old wreck here forever. Besides, the shed belongs to the town. And the town needs it. You've got to get that train out of here." And he marched out.

Dot put her head out of the cab window.

"What are you doing there?" asked Mr. Hobbs.

"We heard Mr. Bodger," said Dot. "What did he mean? Why should you get Number Seven out?"

"They're building a new school halfway to Winslow—a big school. All you kids from miles around are going to it. The town is getting a bus, and they want the shed to keep the bus in."

"But what about Number Seven?" asked Dot.

Mr. Hobbs shook his head. "I reckon it's the end of the line. I'll have to sell her."

Dot looked at her grandpa. She looked at Number Seven. She thought how awful it would be to see the little engine dragged away to be cut up. Suddenly she had an idea.

"Grandpa!" she said. "You know that siding down by the lake where they used to keep extra cars? Number Seven could stay down there. That wouldn't bother anybody."

Mr. Hobbs shook his head. "How are we going to get her down there?"

"Grandpa!" said Dot. "Let's clean her up and run her one more time."

"All right," said Mr. Hobbs. "You kids start on the cars while I take a look at the engine."

Dot ran home and snatched an armful of rags, a broom, and a mop. Back at the train, she and Sam brushed away the mouse nests and the cobwebs. They swept the floor. By suppertime the car looked much better.

Next they started on the engine. That was harder. Then they cleaned the rust off the wheels and the driving rods. They oiled everything. They tested the water tank and filled it. There was a lot of work to do, and it took a long time.

Then the big yellow bus arrived. As there was no shed for it, it stood in Mr. Bodger's yard. Mr. Griggs, the assistant, got the job of driving it. A few days later the new school opened. Mr. Griggs drove the Hogus children to school.

One cold winter afternoon, Dot and Sam saw a crowd of people in front of Mr. Bodger's store. They were looking at a big yellow machine. Mr. Hobbs was there too.

"It's a snowplow," said Mr. Bodger proudly. "The latest thing. It's to clear the road so the school bus can go through."

"Where are you going to keep it?" Mr. Hobbs asked.

"That's a good question," said Mr. Bodger. "We're going to keep it in the shed, right next to the school bus. And that brings me to the next matter, which is that you have till Friday to get that train out of there. The train *and* that pile of coal. That's my last word."

Mr. Hobbs walked back to the train shed.
Dot and Sam hurried after him.

"What'll we do, Grandpa?" Dot asked.

"Got to get her out," said Mr. Hobbs. "Today
is Wednesday. Tomorrow morning I'll fire her
up. Tomorrow afternoon after school we'll
run her out. The pile of coal will have to
set there."

Dot and Sam ran home. They could hardly
wait for Thursday afternoon.

Thursday morning the sky was gray. It
was very cold when Dot woke up. Suddenly
she remembered Grandpa working in the train
shed, getting Number Seven ready for her
last trip.

Dot ran to the shed. Mr. Hobbs was working
on the coal pile, shoveling coal.

"I came to help you," said Dot, grabbing
another shovel.

"All right," said Grandpa. "Let's get the
fire going." Then he looked out through the
open door. It was snowing. Clouds of snowflakes
filled the air.

It snowed all morning, while Mr. Hobbs and Dot worked in the shed. At lunchtime they went home to Grandpa's house for some hot soup. Mr. Hobbs turned on the radio. A voice said, "Travelers' warnings are in effect. An unexpected storm has dumped ten inches of snow in two hours. Schools are closing early."

Her grandpa shook his head. "I don't think we're going anywhere," he said. "Not today."

"But, Grandpa! We have to get her out of there. We have to get her to the siding."

"And how are we going to get back from the siding? Fly?"

"I never thought of that," said Dot, as she turned off the radio.

In the silence, another noise was heard.
They looked out of the window. Mr. Griggs was
trying to get the school bus started. It wouldn't
move. It was snowed in!

Mr. Hobbs ran out. Dot ran after him. Mr.
Bodger came running out of his store. He jumped
into the seat of the snowplow and turned
the key.

"Pretty low on gas," he said, peering at
the dashboard. "Tank's out of gas."

"Get shovels," Mr. Bodger yelled. "Shovel
the road so the school bus can get started."

"Calm down, now, Bodger," said Mr. Griggs.
"We can't shovel the road all the way to
Winslow."

Dot pulled her grandpa's sleeve. "I know where there's a snowplow," she said. "And we don't need gas to run it."

"You're right, Dot," said Mr. Hobbs. "Come on. Griggs, you come too."

They ran to the train shed. In a corner lay Number Seven's plow. Mr. Griggs got the steam going and then he helped Mr. Hobbs hitch the snowplow on the engine. Then all three of them climbed on board.

Dot pulled the cord. *"Clang-clang! Clang-clang!"*

There were shouts from outside. People came running and asked, "What's going on?"

Out of the shed chugged old Number Seven,
with Dot pulling the bell cord and Mr. Hobbs
blowing the whistle. *"Whooo! Whooo! Who-whooo!"*

Mr. Bodger came charging across the road and
demanded, "Where do you think you're going,
Hobbs?"

"Going to get the kids," said Grandpa.

"You have no permit to operate a train!"
shouted Mr. Bodger.

"We'll discuss that later," Mr. Hobbs called
back. "First we have to get things done!"

Number Seven was on her way, her plow
throwing a great curve of snow.

On the steps of the schoolhouse, the Hogus children waited for the bus. But no bus came.

Then, through the drifting snow, they heard a bell and saw a light coming slowly along the track. Teachers and children stared as if they were seeing a ghost. The only one who understood was Sam.

"It's Number Seven!" he yelled.

"Hooray!" everybody cheered. They ran through the deep snow and climbed on board.

"Hi, Mr. Griggs! Hi, Mr. Hobbs! Hi, Dot!" they called joyfully. Slowly, carefully, Number Seven backed all the way home to Hogus. People came running, happy to see their children back.

74

Mr. Bodger was not so happy, and he came striding through the snow to Number Seven. His face was red.

"Well, Bodger," Mr. Hobbs said. "I guess I broke the law. I ran the train without a permit."

Mr. Bodger said, "Yes, you did, but I'll overlook it this time."

"You'll overlook it?" shouted Mr. Hobbs. "Who got these kids home?"

"You can't carry kids without a permit," said Mr. Bodger.

"You mean it's better to leave them there in the snow?" yelled Mr. Hobbs.

Dot and Sam looked at each other. "Wait!" Dot called, but nobody heard her. She had to do something.

"Sam!" she said, "Ring that bell!"

"*Clang-clang!*" went the bell. There was instant quiet. Dot leaned out of the cab and shouted, "I want to speak."

The grown-ups stared at her in surprise.

"I just want to say," said Dot, "that Number Seven got us home. But who's going to get us to school tomorrow?"

"That's only the first snow," said Mr. Griggs. "We've got the whole winter ahead of us. We need the train."

Mr. Bodger looked at the crowd. It seemed he was outnumbered.

"All right, folks," he said. "Tomorrow night we'll have a town meeting."

"No!" the people shouted. "Let's have it right now."

It was the strangest town meeting that ever was held.

Mrs. Beatty made a motion. "Cars are all right, but we need a train too. I move we keep Number Seven."

76

"I second the motion," said Mr. Griggs.

"All in favor say *aye*!" said Mr. Bodger.

"Aye!" came the shouted reply.

"All against." There was no sound but the hissing of snow on the engine.

"The motion is carried," said Mr. Bodger.

Dot, leaning down from the cab, grinned at her grandpa. He gave her a big wink.

"That's the way to get things done," he said.

Comprehension Check

1. What size was Engine Number Seven?
2. Who brought about changes in the small town of Hogus? What were the changes?
3. Why did Mr. Hobbs buy Engine Number Seven? How did he feel about it?
4. How did the people of Hogus feel about Engine Number Seven? Did their feelings change? What finally made the people see that they needed Engine Number Seven?
5. Suppose you had lived in Hogus. What other uses can you think of for Engine Number Seven?

Song of the Train

by David McCord

Clickety-clack,
Wheels on the track,
This is the way
They begin the attack:
Click-ety-clack,
Click-ety-clack,
Click-ety, *clack*-ety,
Click-ety
Clack.

Clickety-clack,
Over the crack,
Faster and faster
The song of the track:
Clickety-clack,
Clickety-clack,
Clickety, clackety,
Clackety
Clack.

I Have a Sister, My Sister Is Deaf

by Jeanne Whitehouse Peterson

I have a sister. My sister is deaf. She is special. There are not many sisters like mine.

My sister can play the piano. She likes to feel the deep rumbling chords. But she will never be able to sing. She cannot hear the tune.

My sister can dance with a partner or march in a line. She likes to leap, to tumble, to roll, to climb to the top of the monkey bars. She watches me as we climb.

I watch her too. She cannot hear me shout "Look out!" But she can see me swinging her way. She laughs and swings backward, trying to catch my legs.

I have a sister who likes to go with me out
to the grassy lot behind our house. Today we
are stalking deer. I turn to speak to her. I use
no voice, just my fingers and my lips.

She understands and walks behind me, stepping
where I step. I am the one who listens for small
sounds. She is the one who watches for quick
movements in the grass.

When my sister was very small, when I went to school and she did not, my sister learned to say some words. Each day she sat on the floor with our mother, playing with some toys we keep in an old shoe box. "It's a ball," our mother would say. "It's a dog. It's a book."

When I came home, I also sat on the floor. My sister put her hands into the box. She smiled and said, "Ball." *Baaaal* it sounded to me. "It's a ball," I repeated, just like our mother did. My sister nodded and smiled. "Ball," she said once more. Again it sounded like *baaaal* to me.

Now my sister has started going to my school, although our mother still helps her speak and lip-read at home. The teacher and children do not understand every word she says, like *sister* or *water* or *thumb*.

Today the children in her room told me, "Your sister said *blue!*" Well, I heard her say that a long time ago. But they have not lived with my sister for five years the way I have.

82

I understand my sister. My sister understands what I say too, especially if I speak slowly and move my hands a lot. But it is not only my lips and fingers that my sister watches.

I wore my sunglasses yesterday. The frames are very large. The lenses are very black. My sister made me take them off when I spoke.

What do my brown eyes say to her brown eyes? That I would really rather play ball than play house? That I just heard our mother call, but I do not want to go in yet?

Yes, I have a sister who can understand what I say.

But not always.

Last night I asked, "Where are my pajamas?" She went into the kitchen and brought out a bunch of bananas from the fruit bowl on the table.

My friends ask me about my little sister. They ask, "Does it hurt to be deaf?"

"No," I say, "her ears don't hurt, but her feelings do when people do not understand."

My sister cannot always tell me with words what she feels. Sometimes she cannot even show me with her hands. But when she is angry or happy or sad, my sister can say more with her face and her shoulders than anyone else I know.

I tell my friends I have a sister who knows when a dog is barking near her and who says she does not like the feel of that sound.

She knows when our cat is purring if it is sitting on her lap, or that our radio is playing if she is touching it with her hand.

But my sister will never know if the telephone is ringing or if someone is knocking at the door. She will never hear the garbage cans clanging around in the street.

I have a sister who sometimes cries at night, when it is dark and there is no light in the hall. When I try plugging my ears in the dark, I cannot hear the clock ticking on the shelf or the television playing in the living room. I do not hear any cars moving out on the street. There is nothing. Then I wonder, is it the same?

I have a sister who will never hear the branches scraping against the window of our room. She will not hear the sweet tones of the wind chimes I have hung up there.

But when the storms come, my sister does not wake to the sudden rolling thunder, or to the quick *clap-clap* of the shutters in the wind. My little sister sleeps. I am the one who is afraid.

86

When my friends ask, I tell them I have a sister who watches television without turning on the sound. I have a sister who rocks her dolls without singing any tune.

I have a sister who can talk with her fingers or in a hoarse, gentle voice. But sometimes she yells so loud, our mother says the neighbors will complain.

I stamp my foot to get my sister's attention, or wave at her across the room. I come up beside her and put my hand on her arm. She can feel the stamping. She can feel the touching. She can glimpse my moving hand from the corner of her eye. But if I walk behind her and call out her name, she cannot hear me.

I have a sister. My sister is deaf.

Comprehension Check

1. What things does the deaf girl watch in order to understand her older sister?
2. How does the deaf girl show people how she feels?
3. Why do you think the deaf girl is not afraid of the storm?
4. What kind of people are the deaf girl's mother and her older sister? Why do you think as you do?
5. Suppose you had a sister who was deaf. What kinds of things would you like to do with her?

Skill Check

Look at each word next to a number. Find the word below it that has the same vowel sound.

1. voice
   a. toy   b. town   c. out
2. light
   a. lid   b. child   c. sit
3. book
   a. look   b. school   c. cool
4. brown
   a. know   b. bowl   c. down

Learning to Pronounce Words

A dictionary can help you pronounce new words correctly. Next to each dictionary word, you will find special symbols in parentheses. Each symbol stands for one of the sounds in the word.

Look at the entry for the word <u>robot</u>.

ro bot (rō′bət), machine made in imitation of a human being; a mechanical device that does routine work in response to commands. See picture. *noun.* [*Robot* comes from a Czech word meaning "work."]

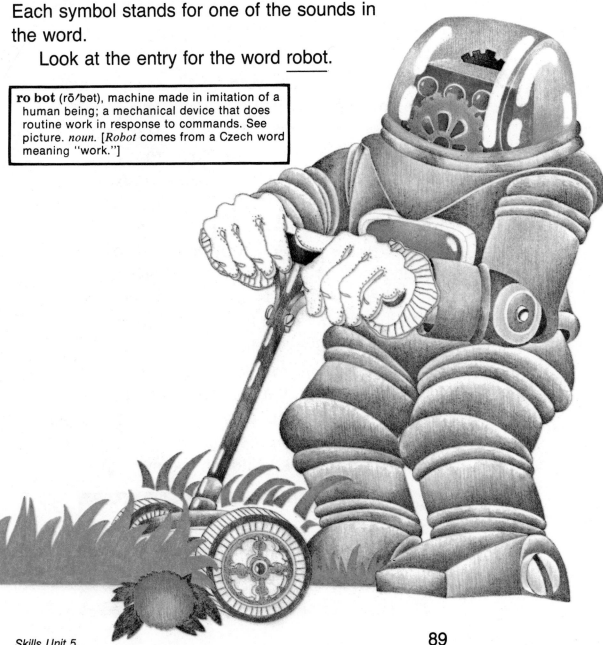

The special symbols that follow the entry word are explained in the pronunciation key. The pronunciation key helps you know the sound that each symbol stands for.

a hat	**i** it	**oi** oil	**ch** child	⌈ a in about
ā age	**ī** ice	**ou** out	**ng** long	e in taken
ä far	**o** hot	**u** cup	**sh** she	ə = ⎨ i in pencil
e let	**ō** open	**u̇** put	**th** thin	o in lemon
ē equal	**ô** order	**ü** rule	**ŦH** then	⌊ u in circus
ėr term			**zh** measure	

There is a sample word next to each symbol in the pronunciation key. The word tells you what sound the symbol stands for. The first two symbols in robot are **ro.** You already know the sound that the symbol **r** stands for. Now look at the word next to the **ō** symbol. The **ō** symbol stands for the **o** sound in open.

Look at the three other symbols in the pronunciation for robot, **bət**. You know the sound that the **b** stands for, and you know the sound that the **t** stands for. Look at the **ə** symbol in the pronunciation key. The symbol is followed by five key words. The symbol **ə** has the same sound as the **a** in about. Look at the other key words for the **ə** symbol. What sound does the **ə** have in those words?

The word robot is written in two syllables.

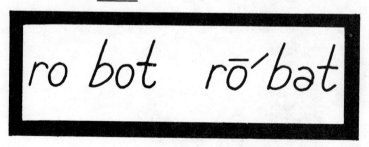

The pronunciation tells you how to say the two syllables. The black mark between the syllables is called an **accent mark**. It tells you which syllable is stressed, or accented. The accent mark comes after the syllable that is accented or stressed. Which syllable is accented in robot?

The ə symbol is in the second syllable. That syllable is not accented. The ə symbol is heard only in syllables that are not stressed or accented.

1. Where can you find out what the pronunciation symbols in a dictionary entry stand for?

2. What are the sample words in the pronunciation key for?

3. What does an accent mark tell you?

Practice

1. Which words in each row have the same beginning sound?

   scene (sēn)　　cheap (chēp)　　cent (sent)
   knot (not)　　　kick (kik)　　　not (not)
   chat (chat)　　chorus (kôr′əs)　check (chek)

2. Which word in each row has an accent on the first syllable?

   cocoon (kə kün′)　　　arrow (ar′ ō)
   grumble (grum′ bəl)　 about (ə bout′)
   exit (eg′ zit)　　　　forty (fôr′ tē)

3. Which syllable is not accented in the words below? Tell why.

   parrot (par ət)　　fortune (for chən)

Use the glossary in the back of this book to help you pronounce new words in the next story about dinosaurs.

F I RODE A DINOSAUR

by Miriam Young

BRONTOSAURUS

I think that giant dinosaurs
Would be such fun to ride,

If only I could figure out
A way to get astride.

When I go to the Museum of Natural History, I like to look at the skeletons of those monsters who lived long, long ago. I keep thinking how great it would be if they were around now. I'd tame them and train them to carry me around on their backs. It might be a little scary but it certainly would be fun.

If I could ride a DIPLODOCUS—the longest dinosaur, as long as three school buses—I'd ride it to the middle of the river and stop. Its head would reach one bank, its tail the other. It'd keep busy nibbling water plants all day, and I'd set up a tollbooth for people who wanted a short cut across the river. A sign would say, "STOP AND PAY TOLL." And at suppertime I'd ride it home again.

It would be neat to ride a PTERANODON, which looks like a giant bat. I'd fly to school and do the loop-the-loop over the school buildings. The children would dash to the windows, and the teachers too. We'd glide and soar and swoop over the playground, and I'd drop leaflets to the teachers from my mother: "Please excuse my child from school this week. The Pteranodon needs exercise."

If I could ride the BRONTOSAURUS—as big as seven elephants!—there'd be room on its back for my whole class! We'd get on its back by climbing an extension ladder, and I'd have my mother make a special harness. We'd all hold on and go thundering through town. We'd wave at people in the top floors of office buildings, but they'd be too surprised to wave back. And on the way home we'd stop at the ball park and see the game—by looking right over the fence.

But the Brontosaurus is so big and heavy, it'd just plod along. So maybe I'd rather ride an ORNITHOMIMUS because it's a fast runner. It looks like an ostrich, but has arms instead of wings and a long tail instead of feathers. It would be great to ride at football practice. My friend Kenny would throw the ball and I'd go dashing down the field on my Ornithomimus. It has long grasping fingers—just perfect for making the catch.

A STYRACOSAURUS would be handy to take on camping trips, and more fun to ride than a bike. I wouldn't have to pack anything. My knapsack, my canteen, my cap, and everything else could just be hooked on its horns. When we got home I'd ride it along our hedge and it would clip the hedge with its strong beak. It would be glad to do it, because to it the hedge would taste just nice and crunchy.

It would be terrific to have a CAMPTOSAURUS to ride in the summer. My friends and I could take turns sliding down its back. I'd tie it up near the wading pool, and while it was nibbling leaves from a nearby tree, we'd go sliding down into the water—splash! It wouldn't mind, I'm sure. That ought to feel like having your back rubbed.

Another dinosaur I'd like to ride is the
TYLOSAURUS, as big as a whale. I'd keep it in
the lake at Grandma's. Most of the time it would
swim underwater. Then suddenly it'd appear—and
disappear again. The newspapers would report,
"MONSTER SIGHTED IN LOCAL LAKE. REAL OR
IMAGINARY?" Then one day I'd swim out and get on
its back and ride it in to shore. Everyone would
rush to take our picture. And we'd appear on
the evening news on TV.

If I had a TRICERATOPS to ride, it would be like having my own private dragon. I'd ride along, sitting just back of its head, and its big bony frill would act like a windshield. It'd be great to take on snowball fights in winter. When a snowball came at me, I could just duck down and never get hit. And I could train it to catch snowballs on its horns.

100

And then there's TYRANNOSAURUS REX, the most ferocious animal that ever lived, with a jaw as big as a steam shovel and teeth like daggers. If I rode Tyrannosaurus Rex, I'd take it to the dentist's and pretend it had a toothache. "Be careful, Dentist," I would say. "It may be feeling fierce today. And when you say 'Open wide,' you might just disappear inside."

I'm sure I'd have a lot of fun
With all these monsters, every one.

Too bad they're not here anymore,
I'd *love* to ride a dinosaur.

Comprehension Check

1. Which dinosaur is a flying dinosaur? How can you tell?
2. How big is the Brontosaurus?
3. Is Tyrannosaurus Rex a plant-eating dinosaur or a meat-eating dinosaur? How can you tell?
4. What is your favorite dinosaur? What would you do with it?
5. If dinosaurs still roamed the world, where might they live? How could they be useful to people?

Skill Check

Use the glossary in the back of this book to answer these questions.

1. How is the word *chameleon* pronounced?
2. Which syllable in the word *chameleon* is accented?
3. Which word in each row has an accent on the first syllable?
   a. imaginary   dagger
   b. locust   ferocious
   c. astride   somersault

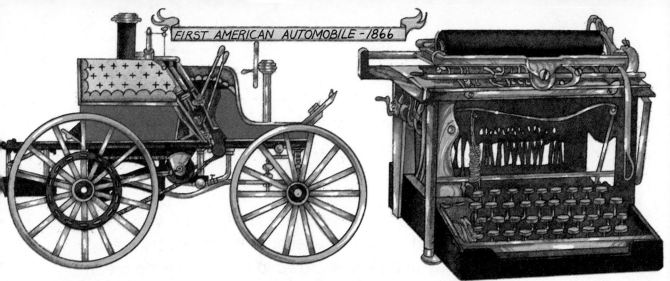
FIRST AMERICAN AUTOMOBILE - 1866

Popular Inventions

TYPEWRITER - 1878

by Webb Garrison

Look around you. There are many things, ordinary things, that we take for granted. Not so long ago, many of these things didn't even exist.

Imagine a world without cars or elevators. Now imagine an ice-cream cone without the cone, or a sleeping bag without zippers. Can you picture streets without traffic lights?

Before we had ice-cream cones or traffic lights, somebody had to invent them. Some inventions were accidental. Others started out as ideas and took years of hard work to become real.

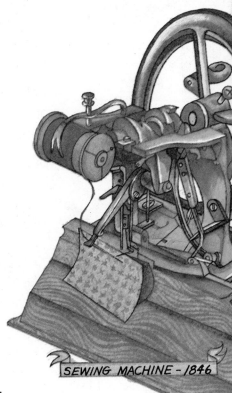
SEWING MACHINE - 1846

Here are some of the most common everyday inventions and the stories of how they came to be.

Ice-Cream Cone

Suppose you were an ice-cream vendor before the ice-cream cone was invented. How would you sell five gallons of ice-cream to one hundred people?

In the middle of August 1904, there was a big fair in St. Louis, Missouri. It was a very hot day and people crowded around the ice-cream cart. The ice-cream vendor, who had been selling ice cream in little dishes, saw that he was quickly running out of dishes. He had to think of something fast.

At that moment, his eyes fell on some crispy, thin wafers from Syria called zalabia. A Syrian friend of his was selling them from the next cart. Thinking quickly, the ice-cream vendor cried, "Give me zalabia!" He rolled up the zalabia, scooped his ice cream on top, and presto! The ice-cream cone was born.

104

Traffic Lights

Suppose you were riding your bicycle down a busy street. What would you do if there were no traffic lights?

A traffic jam with trucks, cars, and buses can be pretty messy. But can you imagine a traffic jam with horses, buggies, and carriages on narrow streets?

Not so long ago a police officer had to stand on each corner and direct traffic. When the car was invented, one officer knew the time had come to solve the problem of traffic jams.

"Railroads have long used signal lights. Why couldn't the same type of lights work as street lights?" thought the officer. Using the red, yellow, and green railroad lights, he made the first traffic lights in 1920.

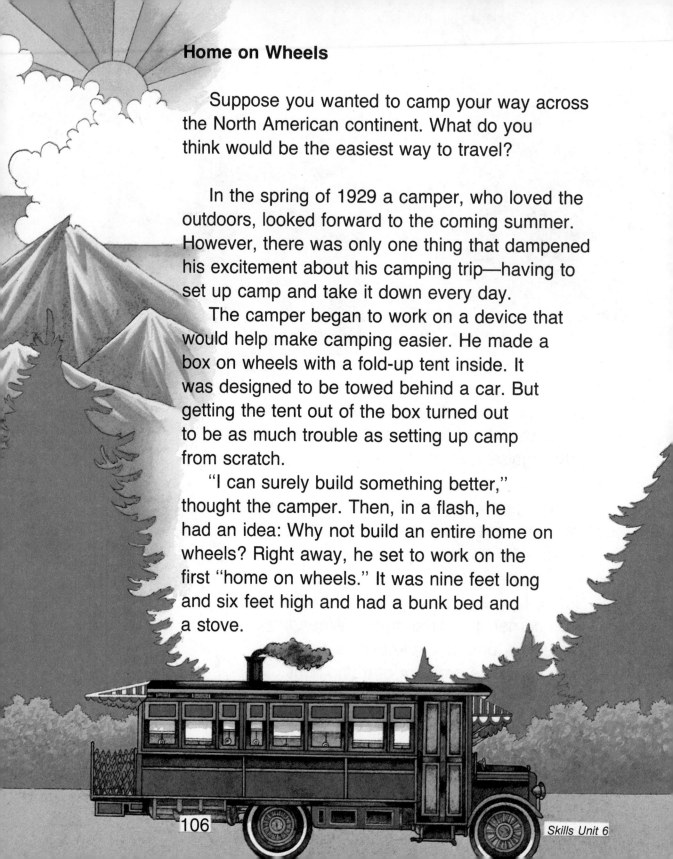

Home on Wheels

Suppose you wanted to camp your way across the North American continent. What do you think would be the easiest way to travel?

In the spring of 1929 a camper, who loved the outdoors, looked forward to the coming summer. However, there was only one thing that dampened his excitement about his camping trip—having to set up camp and take it down every day.

The camper began to work on a device that would help make camping easier. He made a box on wheels with a fold-up tent inside. It was designed to be towed behind a car. But getting the tent out of the box turned out to be as much trouble as setting up camp from scratch.

"I can surely build something better," thought the camper. Then, in a flash, he had an idea: Why not build an entire home on wheels? Right away, he set to work on the first "home on wheels." It was nine feet long and six feet high and had a bunk bed and a stove.

Jigsaw Puzzle

Do you ever wonder what people might do without a jigsaw puzzle on a rainy afternoon?

About two hundred years ago, a geography teacher in London, England, wondered, "How can I help my students learn faster and remember longer?" Instead of regular maps he wanted to use something different.

After much thought, he glued a map of England and Wales to a flat piece of wood. Then, using a very small saw, he cut the map and the wood into pieces following the county lines.

He tried the puzzle with his students. They had fun fitting the pieces together and they learned their geography lesson as well. Soon many kinds of maps and pictures were being made into puzzles for both fun and learning.

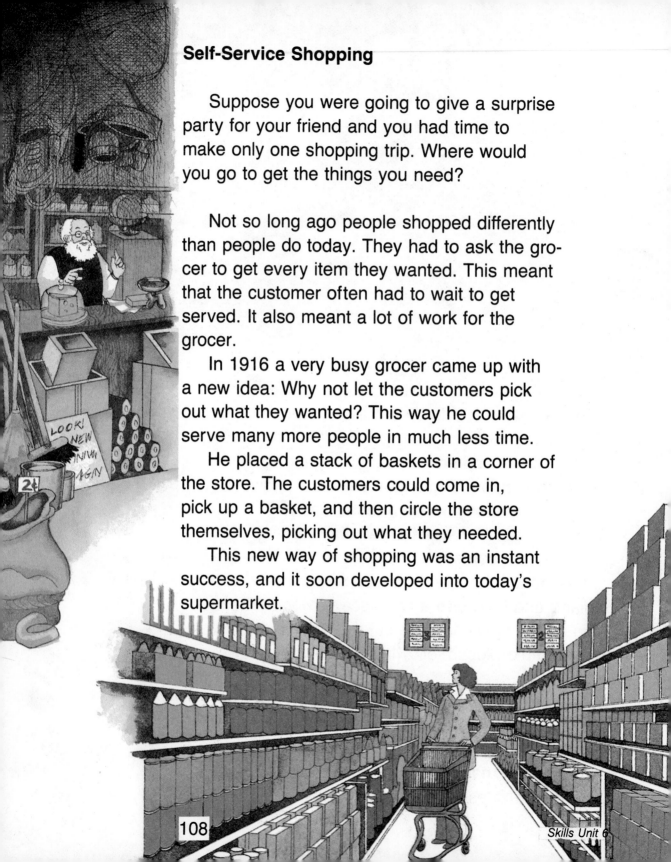

Self-Service Shopping

Suppose you were going to give a surprise party for your friend and you had time to make only one shopping trip. Where would you go to get the things you need?

Not so long ago people shopped differently than people do today. They had to ask the grocer to get every item they wanted. This meant that the customer often had to wait to get served. It also meant a lot of work for the grocer.

In 1916 a very busy grocer came up with a new idea: Why not let the customers pick out what they wanted? This way he could serve many more people in much less time.

He placed a stack of baskets in a corner of the store. The customers could come in, pick up a basket, and then circle the store themselves, picking out what they needed.

This new way of shopping was an instant success, and it soon developed into today's supermarket.

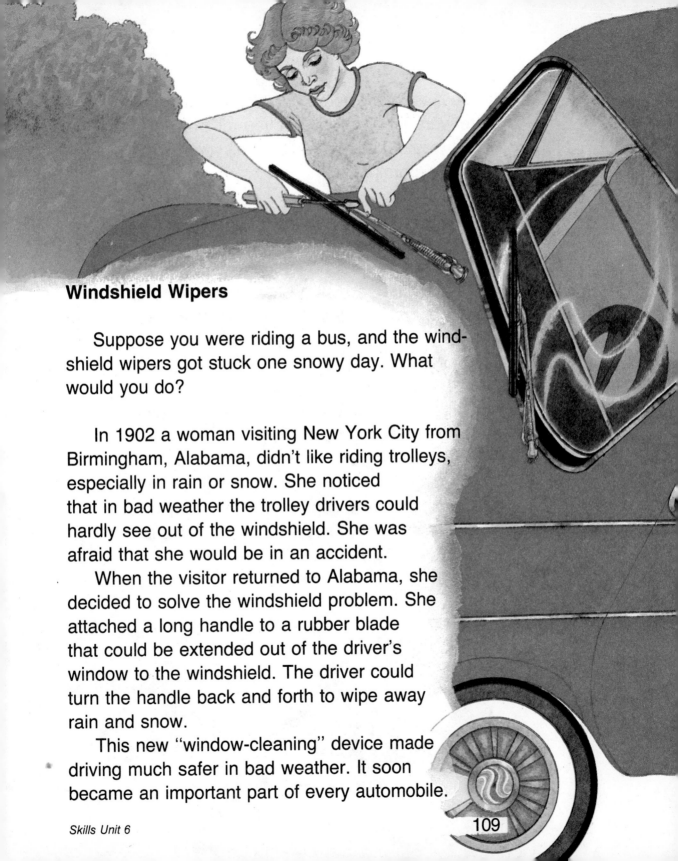

Windshield Wipers

Suppose you were riding a bus, and the windshield wipers got stuck one snowy day. What would you do?

In 1902 a woman visiting New York City from Birmingham, Alabama, didn't like riding trolleys, especially in rain or snow. She noticed that in bad weather the trolley drivers could hardly see out of the windshield. She was afraid that she would be in an accident.

When the visitor returned to Alabama, she decided to solve the windshield problem. She attached a long handle to a rubber blade that could be extended out of the driver's window to the windshield. The driver could turn the handle back and forth to wipe away rain and snow.

This new "window-cleaning" device made driving much safer in bad weather. It soon became an important part of every automobile.

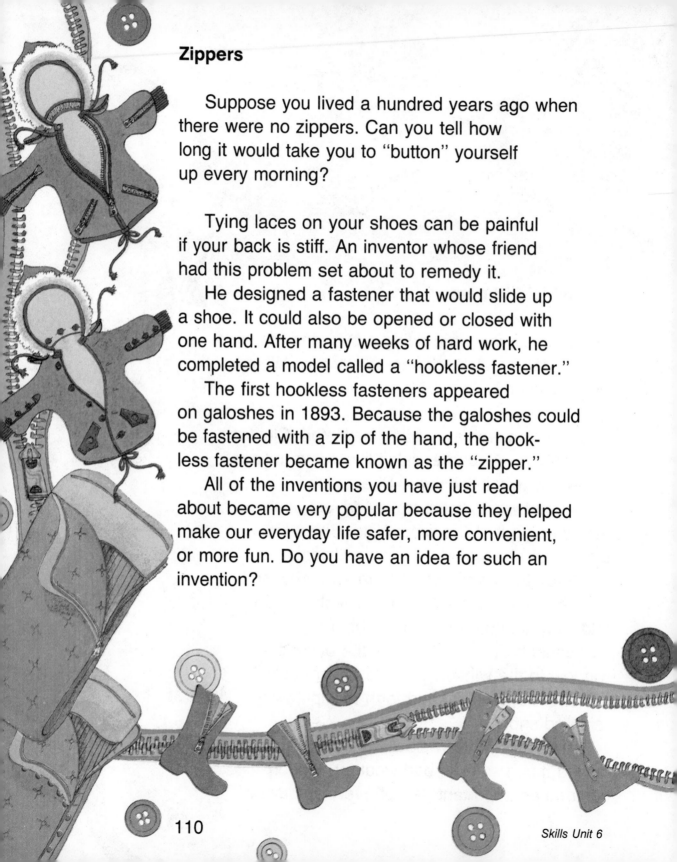

Zippers

Suppose you lived a hundred years ago when there were no zippers. Can you tell how long it would take you to "button" yourself up every morning?

Tying laces on your shoes can be painful if your back is stiff. An inventor whose friend had this problem set about to remedy it.

He designed a fastener that would slide up a shoe. It could also be opened or closed with one hand. After many weeks of hard work, he completed a model called a "hookless fastener."

The first hookless fasteners appeared on galoshes in 1893. Because the galoshes could be fastened with a zip of the hand, the hookless fastener became known as the "zipper."

All of the inventions you have just read about became very popular because they helped make our everyday life safer, more convenient, or more fun. Do you have an idea for such an invention?

Comprehension Check

1. Which invention began in a schoolroom and became something people use at home?
2. What do you think makes an inventor invent things?
3. Do you think the idea of self-service shopping is good? Tell why or why not.
4. Do you have an idea that might lead to an invention? Tell about it.

Skill Check

Read the following paragraph. Then decide which sentence tells the main idea of the paragraph.

The camper began to work on a device that would help make camping easier. He made a box on wheels with a fold-up tent inside. It was designed to be towed behind a car. But getting the tent out of the box turned out to be as much trouble as setting up camp from scratch.

Mr. Hare Takes Mr. Leopard for a Ride

by Carol Korty

Characters:
MR. HARE
MR. LEOPARD
MRS. LEOPARD

MR. HARE *(sitting in front of his house)*:
    Hey, ho, what do you know,
    What shall I do today, today?
    Oh, what shall I do today?
    (MR. LEOPARD rushes by carrying a bucket.)
MR. HARE *(leaps up, delighted)*: Good
    morning, Mr. Leopard! How are you?
MR. LEOPARD: Grrr. . . . *(Throws a glance over his shoulder as he hurries off.)*

MR. HARE: Very nice friend! *(Calls after him.)* You can't even stop long enough to say hello. The only time you are ever friendly to me is when you think you might be able to trick me and catch me for your next meal. Well, it hasn't worked yet. I'm too fast for you. *(Sits again in front of his house.)* Hey, ho, what do you. . . . *(MR. LEOPARD hurries back again.)*

MR. HARE *(leaping up again):* Hey! What do you know! Greetings again, Mr. Leopard!

MR. LEOPARD *(runs across stage without noticing MR. HARE):* Grrr. . . .

MR. HARE: Right in front of my door he passes, and not even a nod! He knows I'm safe in my own territory, so he won't bother with me at all. *(Calls after MR. LEOPARD.)* That's not right! Just because you're big, you should not be rude. At least you can say hello. *(MR. LEOPARD again rushes past, almost knocking over MR. HARE.)*

MR. HARE *(brightly):* Hello! *(Looks after him; realizes it's too late and shrugs. Sits down again.):* Hey, ho, what do you know? What shall I do today? . . . Today! *(He jumps up.)* I know exactly what I'll do today. I'll do something to make that leopard notice me *(looking at audience),* and I don't mean as something to eat! *(He hunches over and walks in a circle with his hands behind his back. He stops and continues to think aloud.)* If his house is that way *(points to where MR. LEOPARD first came in),* and he ran that way *(points to where MR. LEOPARD went out, then looks at audience),* it means he's not home. *(He circles again and then stops.)* I think I'll just take a little walk over to his house and leave a little message. *(MR. HARE circles the stage and stops at MR. and MRS. LEOPARD's house. MRS. LEOPARD is out in front.)* Hello there, Mrs. Leopard.

MRS. LEOPARD: Greetings, Mr. Hare.

MR. HARE: How are you today?

MRS. LEOPARD: Fine, thank you. How are you?

MR. HARE: To tell you the truth, I'm not very well.

MRS. LEOPARD *(concerned):* Oh, I'm sorry to hear that, Mr. Hare.

MR. HARE: Is Mr. Leopard home by any chance?

MRS. LEOPARD: No, he left this morning to go hunting.

MR. HARE: Oh, that's too bad. I needed to use him.

MRS. LEOPARD: Needed to use him? *(Not under-standing.)* What do you mean by that?

MR. HARE: I'm not feeling well, and I want to go to a doctor. It's too long a walk for me feeling this poorly. I thought Mr. Leopard could give a ride.

MRS. LEOPARD *(more puzzled):* What do you mean, "give you a ride"?

MR. HARE: Well, I don't have a horse to ride, so I thought I would ride Mr. Leopard instead.

MRS. LEOPARD *(amused now):* Ride Mr. Leopard?

MR. HARE: Hmmmmm. I'm sure I could do it.

MRS. LEOPARD: It's a good thing for you he isn't around to hear you say that.

MR. HARE *(sure of himself):* I know I could ride him, and I'll bet you I **will** ride him before the day is over. You can tell him that for me, if you will.

MRS. LEOPARD: I just can't believe I'm hearing you right.

MR. HARE: Oh, you're hearing me right. Guess I'll go home and lie down. Good-by, Mrs. Leopard.

MRS. LEOPARD: Good-by, Mr. Hare. And you'd better be more careful.

116

(MR. HARE *leaves slowly, still acting
sick until he is out of MRS. LEOPARD'S
sight. Then he skips merrily home. When
MR. LEOPARD rushes past him toward his
own house, MR. HARE stops short.*)

MR. HARE *(to audience):* Leopards may be big,
but they aren't very bright. *(Runs and
stops short again.)* It's time they
learned their lesson. *(Arrives at his
house.)*

MR. LEOPARD *(rushing on in terrible anger):*
Mr. Hare! Mr. Hare! Mr. Hare!

MR. HARE *(jumping up):* Greetings, Mr. Leopard.
How are you?

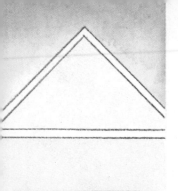

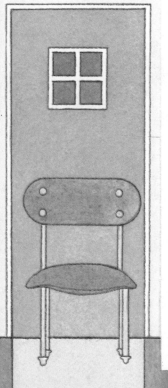

MR. LEOPARD *(confused):* Ah. . . . Greetings. *(Becoming angry again.)* Mr. Hare. . . .

MR. HARE: I saw you several times earlier. Sorry you didn't have time to say hello.

MR. LEOPARD: I was in a hurry. *(Angry, he grabs MR. HARE.)* Listen, Mr. Hare. My wife said you were at my house earlier and boasted you would ride me like a horse.

MR. HARE *(slipping out from his grip):* That's ridiculous, Mr. Leopard!

MR. LEOPARD: It's worse than ridiculous, it's insulting!

(MR. LEOPARD paces up and down, and MR. HARE does the same behind MR. LEOPARD.)

MR. HARE: It's very insulting!

MR. LEOPARD: I'm absolutely furious!

MR. HARE: I would be too!

MR. LEOPARD *(stopping):* Wait, now you're the one who said that. *(MR. HARE gives an innocent shrug.)* My wife said so!

MR. HARE: Maybe your wife was mistaken.

MR. LEOPARD *(circling him and speaking slowly):*
My wife told me very clearly that you
told her to give me the message that
you would ride me like a horse.

MR. HARE: There must be some mistake.

MR. LEOPARD: Now wait a minute. *(He thinks.)*
My wife wouldn't just make up a story
like that. There is no mistake. And no
one is going to make a fool out of me.

MR. HARE: Certainly not, Mr. Leopard.

MR. LEOPARD *(very sure of himself):* I want to hear the two of you straighten this out. Come on home with me. *(He starts to leave.)* I'll ask my wife to repeat the message in front of you.

MR. HARE *(brightly):* I'd really like to come with you, Mr. Leopard *(acting sick again),* but I'm sick today. Didn't Mrs. Leopard tell you?

MR. LEOPARD *(getting angrier):* Come on! You know I live nearby.

MR. HARE *(falling down):* That's true, but I'm feeling weaker every minute.

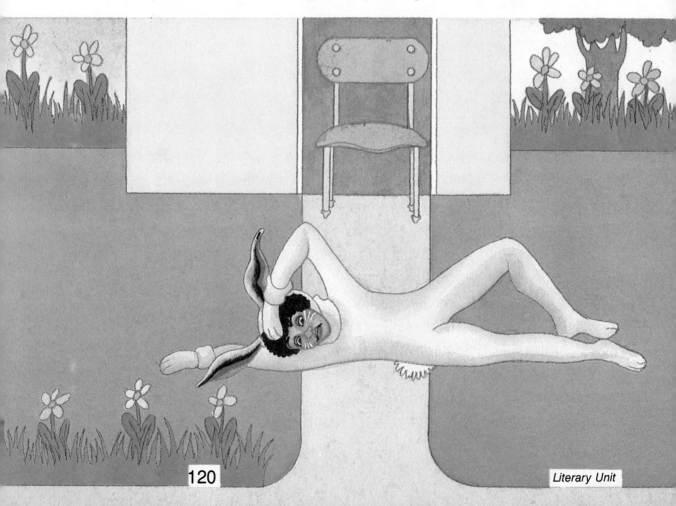

MR. LEOPARD *(furious):* I have been insulted today, and the matter is going to be settled today! Do you hear?

MR. HARE *(weakly):* I don't see why it can't wait until I'm feeling stronger.

MR. LEOPARD: You're coming with me today, even if I have to carry you! *(Grabs MR. HARE's arm and pulls him to his feet.)*

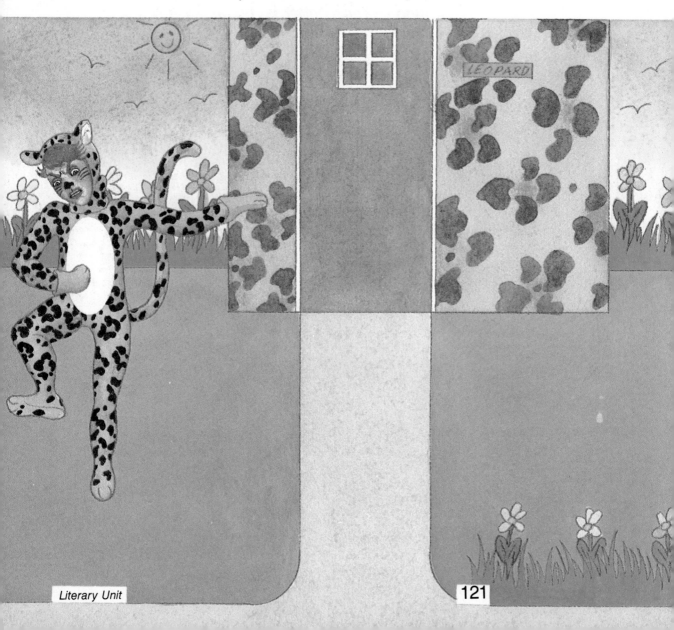

MR. HARE *(weakly):* All right then. You'll have
to carry me; I'm too weak to walk.
(He sinks down again.)

MR. LEOPARD *(thoroughly angry and frustrated):*
Hurry up. Get on my back. *(Bends over.)*

MR. HARE: If you insist! *(Jumps up and stands
with one leg on each side of MR.
LEOPARD's back.)* We're off! *(They
gallop to the Leopards' house.)*

122

MR. HARE: Faster, Mr. Leopard, faster!

    (MRS. LEOPARD comes out of the house.)

    Hello there, Mrs. Leopard!

MR. LEOPARD: We just came by to check up on the boast that Mr. Hare would ride me like a horse.

    (MRS. LEOPARD looks alarmed as MR. LEOPARD slowly straightens up. It dawns on MR. LEOPARD what has happened. MR. HARE slowly slides off his back.)

MR. HARE: Well, I guess I'll be going now. I feel much better. *(Starts moving off.)* Thanks for the ride.

MR. LEOPARD: Like a horse!

(MR. LEOPARD realizes what has happened; he throws MRS. LEOPARD a look and races off, chasing MR. HARE with a roar. Both exit in chase. MRS. LEOPARD exits slowly, shaking her head.)

Comprehension Check

1. How do Mr. Hare and Mr. Leopard get along? What parts of the play tell you?
2. Why did Mr. Hare want to trick Mr. Leopard?
3. What is the trick played on Mr. Leopard by Mr. Hare?
4. Why didn't Mrs. Leopard believe Mr. Hare when he said he would ride Mr. Leopard?
5. Do you think Mr. Leopard deserved to be tricked by Mr. Hare? Tell why or why not.

The Rabbit and the Fox

by Clive Sansom

A RABBIT came hopping, hopping,
Hopping along in the park.
"I've just been shopping, shopping,
I must be home before dark."

A fox came stalking, stalking,
Stalking from under a tree.
"Where are you walking, walking?
Why don't you walk with me?"

The rabbit went hopping, hopping,
Hopping away from the tree.
"I've just been shopping, shopping,
I must be home for my tea."

"Come with me, bunny, bunny—
Bunny, you come with me;
I'll give you some honey, honey,
I'll give you some honey for tea."

"I can't be stopping, stopping,
I'm far too busy today"—
And the rabbit went hopping, hopping,
Hopping away and away.

Finding the Main Idea

Most paragraphs have a main idea. The **main idea** is what the paragraph is about. One sentence in the paragraph usually tells the main idea. The other sentences in the paragraph give details that tell about the main idea.

Read the paragraph below. Find the sentence that tells the main idea. Look for details in the other sentences.

Bees are very helpful insects. Bee hives are our only source of honey. Bees also make wax, which we use to make candles and soap. Many plants need bees too. The bees carry a yellow powder called <u>pollen</u> from plant to plant. The pollen helps the flowers grow.

The main idea of the paragraph on page 126 is stated in the first sentence: <u>Bees are very helpful insects</u>. Do you know why that sentence is the main idea? It tells what the paragraph is about. All the other sentences give details that tell about the main idea. What are some of the details in the paragraph about bees?

Which detail might be added to the paragraph about bees?

a. Bees also help people tell when it is going to rain.

b. A bee will sting you if it is angry.

c. A bee has four wings.

Practice

Read the paragraph below.

Some cities in the United States have unusual names. There is a small town in Alabama called Opp. There are places named Marion, Roy, Murry, and Irving. If you like plants, then Plant City in Florida is just for you. If you travel far enough, you will find two Sandwiches. One is Sandwich, Massachusetts. The other is Sandwich, Illinois.

1. What is the main idea of the paragraph?
2. What are some of the details?

Pay attention to main ideas and details when you read the next story about Benjamin Banneker. The main ideas and details will help you when you read.

BENJAMIN BANNEKER

by Linda Everstz

Young Benjamin Banneker was full of curiosity. What was that object in Joseph Levi's palm? When Benjamin took it up in his hand, he noticed that the thing made a sound—a soft ticking sound. On what was obviously the front side, there were two long stems pointing at different numbers. The thing in his hand was a pocket watch. Joseph Levi knew that Benjamin was fascinated with the watch. But he probably didn't know what Benjamin Banneker was going to achieve with it.

On his way home that night with Joseph
Levi's gift clutched tightly in his hand,
Benjamin thought about his new watch. He
longed to find out what made the ticking
sound. And what did the sound have to do
with the long stems, or hands?

Benjamin hurried home to show his mother
the new possession. She put down her work
when he came rushing in to greet her.
She could tell Benjamin had something very
special to show her.

As she listened, Benjamin told her about
his marvelous watch. He planned to take the
watch apart and learn how it worked inside.
But he was afraid that he wouldn't be able to
put it back together. His mother said,
"Benjamin, if you don't take your watch
apart, you'll never learn how it works.
If you don't figure out how it works,
you'll never be happy."

Working slowly and carefully, Benjamin took apart the watch. How wonderfully each piece fit together! He noticed the way all the cogs and springs and little parts worked in perfect unity. After he studied the parts carefully, he slowly put the watch back together again.

Taking apart the watch wasn't enough for the young man who was anxious to learn and do everything. He wanted to make his own clock. No one had ever made a clock in America without pieces and parts from Europe. For the clock to be his very own creation, Benjamin had to make the parts himself. He carved each wheel and cog by hand from thin wood blocks. Often he had to carve a piece several times to make it fit just the right way. At last the pieces were ready and Benjamin put together his clock. It had taken him two years, but he had made the first entirely American-made clock.

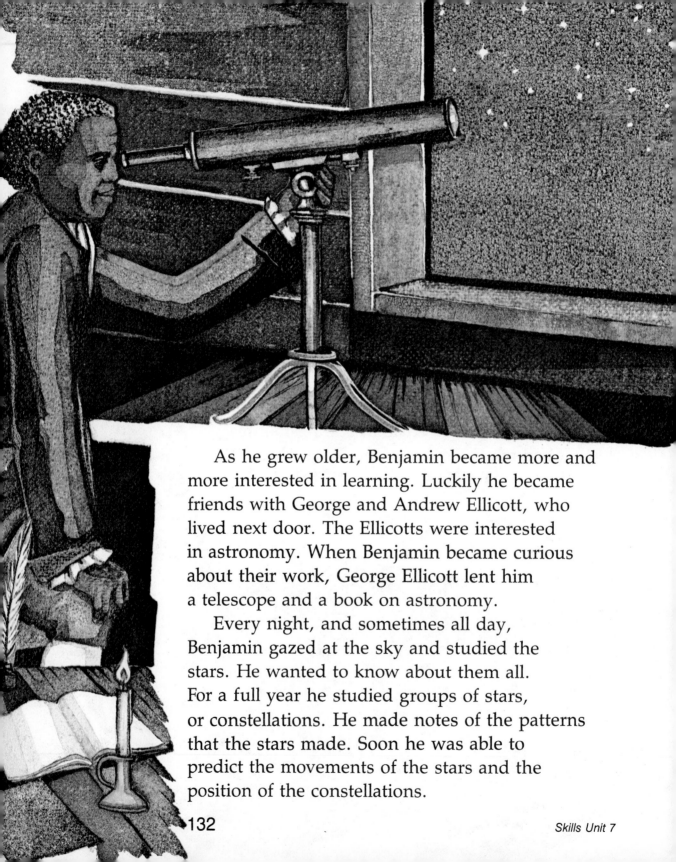

As he grew older, Benjamin became more and more interested in learning. Luckily he became friends with George and Andrew Ellicott, who lived next door. The Ellicotts were interested in astronomy. When Benjamin became curious about their work, George Ellicott lent him a telescope and a book on astronomy.

Every night, and sometimes all day, Benjamin gazed at the sky and studied the stars. He wanted to know about them all. For a full year he studied groups of stars, or constellations. He made notes of the patterns that the stars made. Soon he was able to predict the movements of the stars and the position of the constellations.

132

Andrew Ellicott thought that Benjamin should write an almanac—a book about the weather and stars that is printed each year. Farmers and people who fish could use the book to find out what the weather would be like in the coming months. Benjamin was excited about the idea, and he began to work on the almanac right away.

Benjamin spent a great deal of time working on his almanac. He filled page after page with descriptions of the evening tides. He made lists of herbs that could be used to cure certain illnesses. Benjamin had also found someone who wanted to print his almanac. But suddenly Benjamin was called away on a very special assignment.

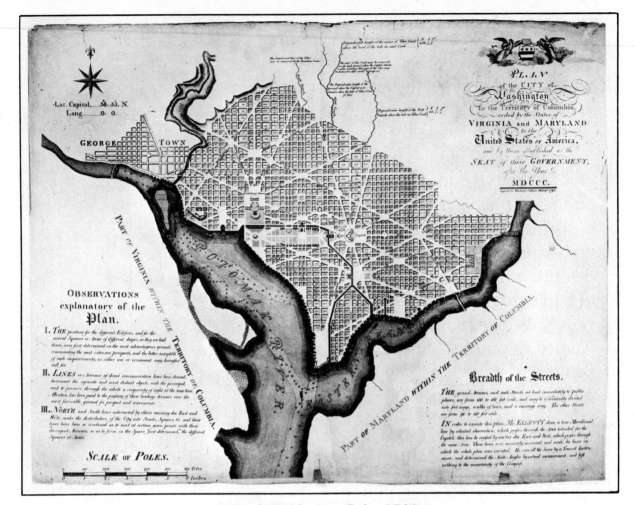

Map of Washington, D.C., 1792

Andrew Ellicott wanted Benjamin to work
with him on an important project. Together
they were going to plan the boundaries of
Washington, D.C.—the future capital of the
United States government. The designs for the
buildings and streets in the city were made
by a Frenchman named Major L'Enfant. The
plans called for the city to have beautiful
wide avenues and streets that branched out
from the Capitol building like spokes from
a wheel.

In 1791 Benjamin and Andrew worked together
to set the boundary lines. They used their knowl-
edge of mathematics and astronomy to make
correct lines from north to south and east to
west. Their work was so admired that President
Washington himself came to praise the two men.

The work on the new city of Washington, D.C., did not go smoothly. Although Major L'Enfant was a good engineer, he was also stubborn and had a bad temper.

A day came when the building planners and Major L'Enfant could no longer work together. Major L'Enfant returned to France and took all the plans and maps with him. The work on Washington, D.C., was called off. "It is a shame that Major L'Enfant's plans should go to waste," Benjamin thought.

Something had to be done. A meeting was called to talk about the plans for building Washington, D.C. Benjamin said that he could remember the major's plans, and he offered to make a new map for the builders to follow. In just two days Benjamin gave the builders the plans and the new map.

Work on the new city started again. Benjamin and Andrew finished their job of helping to build one of the most beautiful capitals of the world. Then Benjamin went home to finish his almanac.

After many weeks of reading, writing, and checking, Benjamin finally completed his almanac in 1792. Every year until 1802 Benjamin Banneker wrote a new almanac, and it was used in almost every American home.

Benjamin Banneker retired to his farm in 1802, just after the printing of his last almanac. However, he continued to study and to develop his inventions. His farm became a meeting place for many famous people who came from all over the world to talk to him.

138

Comprehension Check

1. What did Benjamin do with the watch he received as a gift?
2. What kind of person was young Benjamin? How can you tell?
3. How did Benjamin help build Washington, D.C., after Major L'Enfant went back to France?
4. Have you ever taken something apart to see what the inside was like? Tell what happened.

Skill Check

Read the paragraph below.

Benjamin spent a great deal of time working on his almanac. He filled page after page with descriptions of the evening tides. He made lists of herbs that could be used to cure certain illnesses. Benjamin had also found someone who wanted to print his almanac.

1. What is the main idea of the paragraph?
2. What are some of the details?

THE TREE HOUSE

by Joan M. Harniman

Silence. There was silence for a full two minutes in the backyard of the Chavez family. This was unusual since the whole Chavez family was standing there. And if you knew nine-year-old Rudy, eight-year-old Yolanda, and five-year-old Elmo, you'd say it was *very* unusual.

140

Of course, nothing lasts forever. The silence ended quickly as Rudy, Yolanda, and Elmo each fired off a question at their parents.

"When did you build it?" asked Yolanda, who couldn't believe that her parents could surprise her like this.

"How did you build it?" Rudy wanted to know as he looked up at the big trees in the yard.

"Who is it for?" asked Elmo, whose eyes were still glued to it.

"Hold on," said Dad. "Give your mom and me a chance to answer. We built the tree house as a surprise for all three of you. I've been looking at these four aspen trees for a long time now. I knew they'd be the perfect four corners for the floor of a great tree house."

"So, this weekend, while you and your grandparents were enjoying the state fair, we were busy," Mom explained.

"That's why you didn't come to the fair with us," said Rudy. "Gramps started to say something about what you and Mom were doing, but then he stopped in a hurry."

"I remember," shouted Elmo. "That was when Gram stepped on his foot."

"Well, your grandparents knew all about the surprise," said Mom with a laugh. "We've been planning it for weeks. The tree house is officially open. You'll all have to share it, but that shouldn't be hard."

"It will be easy," said Elmo as he rushed to be the first to climb up into it.

Yolanda followed him up the wooden ladder that rested securely against the tree house. Rudy raced for the rope ladder that hung from the window. For once they all agreed; the tree house *was* great. The room was a large square with a bench against each wall. A wooden table stood in the center of the room. The tree house had a porch that overlooked the Chavez yard and many other yards in their neighborhood.

142

"Wait till my friends see this!" exclaimed Yolanda. "They'll love to play here!"

"Mine too," thought Rudy.

"What are we waiting for?" Elmo said as he carefully walked down the wooden ladder.

"Now the fun begins," said Dad as he and Mrs. Chavez turned back to their house.

Well, Mr. Chavez wasn't exactly right. It all depends on what you call fun. It really started out as fun, but it ended up to be more like trouble. . . .

About fifteen minutes later, ten children were sitting in the tree house. It was an instant hit. They had climbed up the wooden ladder, run out to look at the view from the porch, and scurried down the rope ladder.

Rudy and his two friends were talking excitedly about what they always talked about—rocks. They discussed the name, color, shape, and size of every rock they found. All at once they came out of the tree house. They were in a hurry to do something.

Yolanda and her two friends were in another world. They were space explorers, on the lookout for alien beings from another planet. Yolanda said something about getting into their land cruiser, and off they went.

Elmo and his three friends hardly noticed. They were making big decisions. They were deciding what super heroes they would be for the day. Each day they all saved at least one person from danger. On a good day, they rescued cities, and once they saved the world itself. Suddenly the four super heroes seemed to disappear from the tree house.

Eight minutes later, the trouble began. The rock hunters were lugging their precious bags of newly found rocks to the Rock Room.

At that same time, the space crew was racing toward an alien spaceship that had just landed. It was their mission to board the ship, which looked strangely like the new tree house.

And at that very same time, the super heroes were running to save some helpless people. Their capes were flying behind them. The Bird Monster had scooped the people up into her nest in the new tree house.

Suddenly, super hero Elmo tripped on his cape and fell into space explorer Yolanda. Yolanda collided with rock hunter Rudy, who dropped his bag of rocks on his foot.

"Where do you think you're going?" shouted Rudy. "We're using the tree house as our Rock Room now."

"Who said?" Yolanda shouted back. "The tree house is a spaceship, and it's ours right now."

"Well, what's going to happen to the poor people in the Bird Monster's nest?" cried Elmo.

Yolanda gave Elmo a playful hug as he burst out laughing. Soon the rock hunters, space explorers, and super heroes were all laughing.

"OK," said Rudy. "We have a problem. What can we do about it?"

"Well . . ." Yolanda thought out loud, "Mom and Dad told us the tree house was ours to share. How do you share a tree house?"

"I know," said Elmo. "Each club gets a bench in the tree house."

"Oh, no!" disagreed Yolanda. "We all can't be in the tree house at the same time. It would get too crowded."

"And too painful," said Rudy, rubbing his foot.

"Let's see," said Yolanda. "When would you like to study rocks in the tree house, Rudy? And how much time do you need?"

"We always get together early Saturday morning," said Rudy, "right after breakfast. That's when we look at the rocks we have and decide which rocks to look for."

146

"All right. So the rock hunters can use the
tree house for the first hour. Then my space club
can use it for the next hour."

"And then the super heroes have an hour,"
said Elmo.

"It just might work, Yolanda," said Rudy.

"You know what we're doing?" said Yolanda
excitedly. "We're making up a tree house
schedule. I'll go get the paper and pencils,
and I'll meet you in the tree house. We can draw
up a tree house schedule right there."

148

This is what their schedule looked like:

Tree-house Schedule

After School (weekdays)

3:00-3:30	Super heroes
3:30-4:00	Space explorers
4:00-4:30	Rock hunters
4:30-5:00	Clean up (all club members)

Saturday

9:00-10:00	Rock hunters
10:00-11:00	Space explorers
11:00-12:00	Super heroes
12:00-1:00	Lunch
1:00-2:00	Rock hunters
2:00-3:00	Space explorers
3:00-4:00	Super heroes
4:00-5:00	Clean up (all club members)

Sunday

12:00-1:00	Lunch
1:00-2:00	Rock Show
2:00-3:00	Spaceship Exhibition
3:00-4:00	Super Heroes' Play
4:00-5:00	Clean up (all club members)

Their schedule was a good one. The club members themselves were a little surprised that it worked so well. Rudy's foot got better, and there were no more accidents. The hunters, heroes, and explorers had to agree that their schedule made it easy to share the tree house.

Comprehension Check

1. When did Mr. and Mrs. Chavez build the tree house?
2. How did they keep it a secret from the children?
3. What kind of club did each of the Chavez children belong to?
4. How did the children solve the problem of sharing the tree house? Do you think it was a good solution? Tell why or why not.
5. Suppose you had to share a club house with some of your friends. What kind of schedule would you make?

Skill Check

Use the tree-house schedule on page 149 to answer each question below.

1. When do the rock hunters get to use the tree house on a weekday afternoon?
   a. 4:30–5:00   b. 3:30–4:00   c. 4:00–4:30
2. Which club gets to use the tree house from 11:00 to 12:00 on a Saturday?
   a. super heroes   b. rock hunters
   c. space explorers
3. What event takes place at the tree house from 1:00 to 2:00 on a Sunday?
   a. Super Heroes' Play   b. Rock Show
   c. Spaceship Exhibition
4. How long do the children take to clean up the tree house on a weekday?
   a. half hour   b. one hour   c. two hours

Recognizing Root Words, Suffixes, and Endings

A suffix or ending can be added to many words. You have already seen endings like er in bigger and en in broken. Other endings you may know are s, es, ed, ly, est, and ing. You have also seen suffixes like less in spotless and ful in careful. Other suffixes you may know are er as in teacher, and y as in lucky.

A suffix or ending is added to a root word. The root word in cheerful is cheer. The root word in sleeping is sleep. What is the root word in smartest? What is the ending?

1. Sometimes the root word does not change when the ending or suffix is added. The suffix or ending is just added to the end of the word. What are the root words in building, jumping, quickly, peaches, snowy, sixth, and bricks?

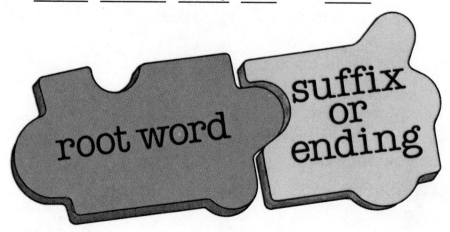

2. Sometimes the root word changes before a suffix or ending is added:

   a. The final consonant in the word may be doubled. What are the root words in <u>popping</u>, <u>running</u>, and <u>stopping</u>? What consonants are doubled?

   b. Sometimes the final e of a root word is dropped before a suffix or ending is added. What are the root words in <u>noisy</u>, <u>smoky</u>, <u>baked</u>, and <u>driving</u>?

   c. The y at the end of a root word may change to i before a suffix or ending is added. What are the root words in <u>happiest</u>, <u>merrily</u>, <u>busiest</u>, and <u>sillier</u>?

   d. The f at the end of a root word may change to v before a suffix or ending is added. What are the root words in <u>leaves</u>, <u>shelves</u>, <u>loaves</u>, and <u>knives</u>?

Practice

What is the root word in each word below? Does the root word change before the suffix or ending is added? If it does, tell how.

1. classes
2. edging
3. winning
4. shapeless
5. wonderful
6. quickly
7. makes
8. knives
9. shiny
10. cracked
11. woolen
12. thinner
13. eaten
14. heaviest
15. hiding

As you read the next story, "The Shoeshine Chair," you may see a word you don't know. Check to see if the word has a suffix or ending. If you know the root word, you may be able to figure out the meaning of the whole word.

The Shoeshine Chair

by Janice May Udry

One of Angie's favorite places was the second-hand store. The sign in front said "Antiques and Junk for Sale." The old store had three rooms. The front room contained expensive furniture and dishes, but items in the second room cost less. The junk was in the third room. Some things in the junk room cost less than a dollar. The junk room overflowed into a weedy fenced-in junk-yard in the back.

Angie went to the second-hand store hoping to find an unusual but inexpensive present for her father's birthday.

"Have you got any really good junk today, Mr. Whitaker?" asked Angie.

"Sure I have, Angie. Just look around. There's a little bit of everything out there in back," said Mr. Whitaker from behind his cluttered, dusty old desk.

Angie poked around the store for a long time, but she didn't see anything that seemed exactly right for her father's birthday. Before she left she decided to take one last turn around the junkyard.

There, lying on its side, she found something that really interested her. It was an old homemade wooden shoeshine chair. A thin straight chair had been nailed to a large box with a drawer in it. The drawer pulled open with a spool. The chair and the box were nailed to a platform with two wooden footrests on it. The whole thing had been painted sky blue. It was all loose and rickety now.

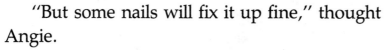

"But some nails will fix it up fine," thought Angie.

"How much for the shoeshine chair?" Angie asked Mr. Whitaker.

"You found one of my best pieces of junk," said Mr. Whitaker. "How much money have you got?"

"Fifty cents," said Angie.

"It's a deal," said Mr. Whitaker. "The shoeshine chair is yours. I'll tell Joe to deliver it to your house."

That afternoon Mrs. Lee answered the doorbell.

"Where do you want this, ma'am?"

"What is it?" asked Mrs. Lee.

"It's your shoeshine chair, ma'am," said Joe.

"I think you have the wrong address. Wait a minute. Angie!"

Angie came to the hall. "That's mine, Mother. Just leave it on the porch, please."

Joe put the chair down and went back to his truck.

"Angie! Is that what you got your father for his birthday?" asked Mrs. Lee.

"No," said Angie. "I didn't find anything yet. I bought this for myself. I know it looks rickety right now, but I'll work on it."

"It makes our front porch look really different," said Mrs. Lee.

"It has a lot of possibilities," said Angie.

Angie was very pleased when she had made the old chair sturdy again with nails. It made a wonderful throne. Angie made herself a crown and dressed up like a queen. She put her royal jewels and valuable papers in the drawer.

When Molly came over with her skates, Angie had an idea.

"Hey, Molly, let's put this throne on wheels."

In a little while, Angie and Molly were pushing each other up and down the street in a strange-looking, high wheelchair. They had nailed their skates to the bottom of the shoeshine chair.

"That was one of my best ideas," said Angie later, when they sat resting on the front steps. "But I still haven't bought a present for my father, and his birthday is the day after tomorrow. I spent all the money I had on the shoeshine chair. I know what I'd like to buy him if I had two dollars."

"What?" asked Molly.

"Have you ever been in the new Gourmet Shop?" asked Angie. "Do you know that they have jars of fried grasshoppers there? That's what I'd like to buy. He's never had that and he'd never guess what it was. Wouldn't it be fun to taste a fried grasshopper?"

"Oh, Angie!" Molly made a face.

"But I haven't got two dollars," said Angie.
For a while she was deep in thought.

"Come on, Angie. Let's take turns riding in
the chair again," said Molly.

"OK," said Angie, getting up.

The young twins next door ran out when they
saw Angie pushing Molly past their house.

"Angie! Angie! Where did you get that? Can we
have a ride?" they begged.

After Angie and Molly had given the twins
a ride, they didn't want to get out of the chair.

"Please give us another ride! It's fun."

"No more today," said Angie.

"Please!"

Angie's face suddenly brightened. "No more
free rides. Have you got any money?"

The twins nodded vigorously.

"Well," said Angie, "for five cents I'll give you a ride all the way around the block."

"OK!" The twins dashed away. "Stay there. We'll be right back!"

Angie grinned at Molly. "Do you know what we're going to do?"

"What?"

"Earn the money for my father's present," said Angie.

"How much do you think the twins have?" asked Molly.

"Not just them. We'll give anybody who wants it a ride for five cents," said Angie. "Wait here with the chair a minute. I'll be right back."

Angie ran home and came back with a small can of paint and a brush. On both sides of the box under the chair she wrote: "Ride—5¢"

As they pushed the twins around the block other children appeared. Like magic they ran into their homes and popped out again with nickels in their hands. Some of them rode more than once.

By dinnertime Angie and Molly were very tired, since some of their riders had demanded fast rides.

"We have to go home now," they told some of the waiting customers. "But we'll be out tomorrow."

Angie and Molly pushed the chair home and into Angie's garage. They counted almost a dollar.

"We'll make another dollar easy," said Angie. "See you tomorrow, Molly. Go to bed early so you won't be tired tomorrow."

"I feel like going to bed right now," said Molly.

Angie grinned. "Remember you're invited to my father's birthday dinner. And you'll get to taste fried grasshoppers, Molly!"

The next morning Angie and Molly added a parasol and a bell to the chair ride. Many of the small children liked the ride even better when they could sit up high under the parasol ringing a bell, while being pushed along the sidewalk.

By the middle of the afternoon Angie and Molly had plenty of money for the present. Angie's mother drove the girls down to the Gourmet Shop.

"I always like to go in here," said Angie. "People look as if they are enjoying themselves and they aren't in any hurry. They're usually in a good mood, I've noticed."

Angie led Molly into the store and down one aisle.

"Here it is," said Angie. "See, you get quite a big can of grasshoppers for two dollars."

"I wonder what my father would say if I gave him fried grasshoppers for his birthday," said Molly with a giggle.

"It's a nice change from neckties," said Angie.

That night Angie gave her father the present.

"This feels like a can of my favorite peanuts," said Mr. Lee.

He untied the ribbon and took off the paper. "Grasshoppers! Fried grasshoppers," cried Mr. Lee with delight. "I have always wanted to taste them." He selected a grasshopper and passed the can. "Help yourselves," he said. "This is a very special treat."

There was a moment of silence while they held
their grasshoppers between thumb and forefinger.

They all waited for someone to take the first
bite.

"Don't they look yummy?" said Mrs. Lee.

"Oh, they certainly do," said Mr. Lee,
gazing intently at his grasshopper.

Molly giggled nervously.

"OK, everybody, one, two, three," Angie said
and popped her grasshopper into her mouth. So did
Mr. and Mrs. Lee. And after taking a deep breath,
so did Molly.

They munched in silence, watching each other's
faces.

"They are very crunchy," said Mr. Lee. He
ate another one.

"I believe I prefer potato chips," said Mrs. Lee.

"We're just not used to the idea of eating grasshoppers," said Angie. "In some countries it's just a plain, ordinary, everyday thing to eat grasshoppers."

"My brother will never believe me when I tell him that I ate a grasshopper," said Molly. "May I take him one?"

"Help yourself," said Mr. Lee.

"Take several," said Mrs. Lee. "There are plenty."

"Thank you for such an unusual present, Angie," said Mr. Lee.

"You're welcome," said Angie with a grin.

166

Comprehension Check

1. What thing in Mr. Whitaker's store did Angie like? Tell what it looked like.
2. What did Angie make out of the shoeshine chair? How did she do it?
3. What kind of a person is Angie? How can you tell?
4. Do you think Angie's way of making money was a good one? Tell why you think as you do.
5. How did Angie's father feel about his present?
6. Fried grasshoppers are an unusual food. What other unusual kind of food can you think of?

Skill Check

What is the root word in each word below? Does the root word change before the suffix or ending is added? If it does, tell how.

1. weedy
2. usually
3. dishes
4. decided
5. wooden
6. crunchy
7. riding
8. wonderful
9. hoping
10. suddenly

The Emperor's New Clothes

by Hans Christian Andersen

Once upon a time there was an emperor who
loved new clothes. He didn't care about his
army, he didn't like to go to the theater,
and he wouldn't even take a ride in the park
unless he had a new costume to show off. He
had a different suit for every hour of the day.

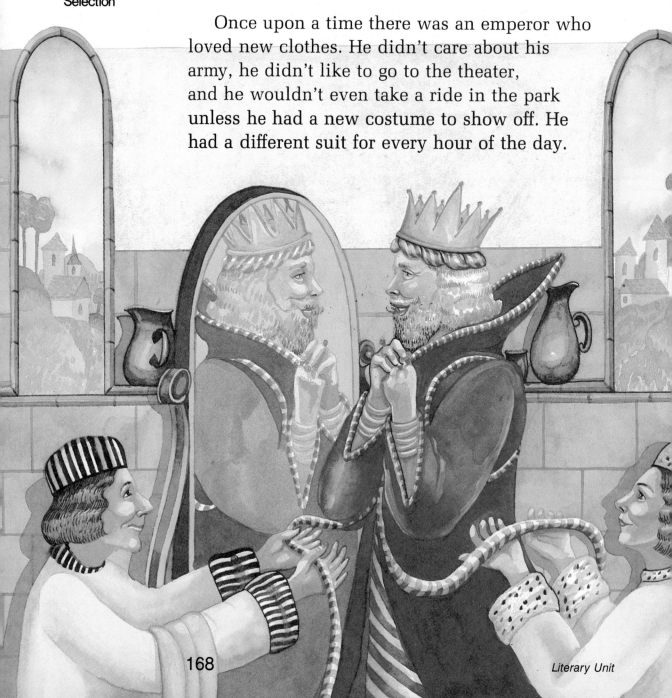

168

The emperor lived in a big, busy city; many strangers passed through there. One day two swindlers came to town who told everyone that they were weavers and that they could weave the most beautiful cloth in the world. And what was more, they said that the cloth had a magical power—it was invisible to anyone who was stupid or unfit for office.

"That cloth would be very useful to me," the emperor thought. "If I had some of it, I could find out which of my people are clever and which are fools. I think I'll have those weavers make me some."

The weavers set up their looms upon the emperor's command. They asked for the finest silk thread and the most expensive gold. They said they needed it to make the cloth. But really they hid it in their suitcases. Then they sat down at the empty looms and pretended to weave.

After a while the emperor wondered how they were getting on. "I'd like to know how much of the cloth is ready," he thought, but he also thought about the fact that a stupid or foolish person wouldn't be able to see the cloth. He was sure that *he* would be able to see it, but he didn't want to take any chances. So he asked himself, "Who can I send to look at the cloth?"

The emperor had an idea. "I know," he said, "I'll send my old chief minister. He's very clever and full of common sense. So he'll be able to tell me what the cloth is like."

So the old minister went to see the cloth. He entered the workroom where the two weavers were pretending to work.

"Oh, my goodness!" the minister thought when he saw the looms. "I can't see a thing!" When he peered harder through his spectacles, he still couldn't see anything, but of course he didn't say so.

"Come closer," the two swindlers said. "Isn't this cloth beautiful?" The old minister looked as hard as he could, but he still couldn't see anything, which was not surprising, because there was nothing to see.

"This is terrible," the old minister thought. "This must mean that I'm a fool! I'd better not let anybody know that I can't see the cloth."

So the old minister nodded his head and said, "It's beautiful. What a wonderful pattern and what marvelous colors! I shall be sure to tell this to the emperor."

Soon everyone in town was talking about the wonderful cloth that the weavers were making. And the emperor decided that he wanted to go and see it for himself. So with a large group of friends and courtiers, he went to the workroom where the weavers sat at their empty looms.

"What's this?" the emperor thought when he saw the looms. "I can't see anything! How awful! Am I a fool, or am I not fit to be emperor? That would be the worst thing that could happen to me!"

But aloud he said, "Oh, it's marvelous, it's beautiful! It's the most wonderful cloth I've ever seen, and I must have a suit made from it right away to wear in the court procession next week!"

All the emperor's friends and courtiers
stared at the looms and nodded—not one of them
would admit that there was nothing to be seen.
Each one of them thought that everyone else
could see the beautiful cloth. "How marvelous,"
they echoed the emperor. "How beautiful!"

So that night the swindlers set to work to make the emperor's new suit. They pretended to roll out the cloth. They cut through the air with big scissors, and they sewed all night with no thread at all in their needles.

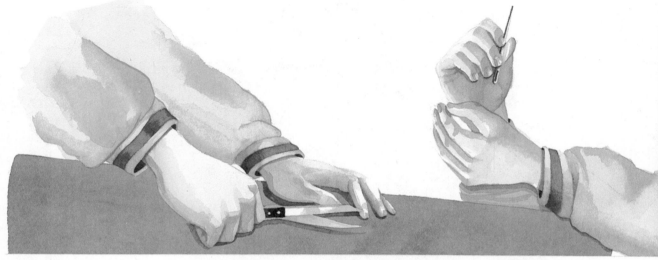

Finally they said that the suit was finished. "Look how beautiful it is," the swindlers said. "And the cloth is so light. When you wear this suit, it will feel like you're wearing nothing at all. Come, your Majesty, and try it on."

The swindlers helped the emperor take off his old clothes. Then, with great care, they helped him put on the new suit. They pretended to put a pin in here and take a tuck in there. Then they pretended to fasten on the long train.

The emperor turned this way and that in front of the mirror, pretending to admire the new suit. "How beautiful it is," all his friends and courtiers said. "How well it fits! You look marvelous, your Majesty!"

Soon it was time for the court procession to
begin. The two attendants who were to carry the
train bent down and pretended to pick it up.
They held their hands high as if they didn't
want the train to touch the floor.

And so the procession started down the main
street of the city. All the people lined the
sidewalks, waiting to see the emperor's new
clothes. As the procession went by, they all
clapped and cheered. "What beautiful clothes!"
the people cried. They wouldn't admit to
anyone that they couldn't see the clothes.

The emperor was very happy. Nothing he had ever worn had met with such approval. He held his head up high.

Then a little child's voice was heard in the crowd. "But the emperor has nothing on," the child said.

At first no one else said anything. Then all the people began to whisper, "The emperor has nothing on."

The emperor felt a chill go down his spine. It suddenly seemed to him that the people were right. He *was* a fool, after all.

"But this procession has started, and it must finish," the emperor thought. He held his head even higher and marched on down the street, and the attendants behind him held on even tighter to the train that wasn't there.

SECTION TWO

Yagua Days

by Cruz Martel

It was drizzling steadily on the Lower East Side of New York City. From the doorway of his parents' grocery store, Adan Riera watched a car splash the sidewalk.

School had ended for the summer two days before, and for two days it had rained. Adan wanted to play in East River Park, but with so much rain, about the only thing a boy could do was watch cars splash by.

Of course he could help his father. Adan enjoyed working in the store. He liked the smells of the fruits and the different colors of the vegetables, and he liked the way the mangoes and ñames felt in his hands.

But today he would rather be in the park. He watched another car spray past. The rain began to fall harder.

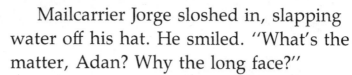

Mailcarrier Jorge sloshed in, slapping water off his hat. He smiled. "What's the matter, Adan? Why the long face?"

"Rainy days are terrible days."

"No—they're wonderful days. They're yagua days!"

"Stop teasing, Jorge. Yesterday you told me the vegetables and fruits in the store are grown in panel trucks. What's a yagua day?"

"This day is a yagua day. And Puerto Rican vegetables and fruits *are* grown in trucks. Why, I have a truck myself. Every day I water it!"

Adan's mother and father came in from the back.

"Hello, Jorge. You look wet."

"I feel wetter. But it's a wonderful feeling. It's a yagua-day feeling!"

His mother and father liked Jorge. They had all grown up together in Puerto Rico.

"So you've been telling Adan about yagua days?" said his father.

"*Si*. Look! Here's a letter for you from Corral Viejo, where we all had some of the best yagua days," said Jorge.

Adan's father read the letter. "Good news! My brother Ulise wants Mami, Adan, and me to visit him on his plantation for two weeks."

"You haven't been to Puerto Rico in years," said Mailcarrier Jorge.

"Adan's never been there," replied his mother. "We can ask my brother to take care of the store. Adan will meet his family in the mountains at last."

Adan clapped his hands. "Puerto Rico! Who cares about the rain!"

Mailcarrier Jorge smiled. "Maybe you'll even have a few yagua days. Have fun, Adan!"

Uncle Ulise met them at the airport in Ponce. "Welcome to Puerto Rico, Adan."

Uncle Ulise had tiny blue eyes in a round, red face, and big, strong arms. But Adan, excited after his first plane ride, hugged Uncle Ulise even harder than Uncle Ulise hugged him.

"Come, we'll drive to Corral Viejo." He winked at Adan's father. "I'm sorry you didn't arrive yesterday. Yesterday was a wonderful yagua day."

"You know about yagua days too, Uncle Ulise?"

"Sure. They're my favorite days."

"But wouldn't today be a good yagua day?"

"The worst. The sun's out!"

In an old jeep, they wound up into the mountains.

"Look!" said Uncle Ulise, pointing at a river. "Your mother and father, Mailcarrier Jorge, and I played in that river when we were children."

They bounced up a hill to a cluster of bright houses. Many people were outside.

"This is your family, Adan," said Uncle Ulise.

Everyone crowded around the jeep. There were old and young people, blond-, brown-, and black-haired people. There were dark-skinned and light-skinned people, blue-eyed, brown-eyed, and green-eyed people. Adan had not known there were so many people in his family.

Uncle Ulise's wife Carmen hugged Adan and kissed both his cheeks. Taller than Uncle Ulise and very thin, she carried herself like a soldier. Her straight mouth never smiled—but her eyes did.

The whole family sat under wide trees and ate rice with peas, roast pork, and salad made with tomatoes and avocados.

Adan talked and sang until his voice turned to a squeak. He ate until his stomach almost popped a pants button.

Afterward he fell asleep under a big mosquito net before the sun had even gone down behind the mountains.

In the morning Uncle Ulise called out, "Adan, everyone ate all the food in the house. Let's get more."

"From a store?"

"No, from my plantation on the mountain."

"You drive a tractor and plow on the mountain?"

Aunt Carmen smiled with her eyes. "We don't need tractors and plows on our plantation."

"I don't understand."

"Come. You will."

Adan and his parents, Aunt Carmen, and Uncle Ulise hiked up the mountain, walking beside a splashy stream.

Near the top they walked through groves of fruit trees.

"Long ago your grandfather planted these trees," Adan's mother said. "Now Aunt Carmen and Uncle Ulise pick what they need for themselves. Or they pick what they want to give away or sell in Ponce."

"Let's work!" said Aunt Carmen.

Sitting on his father's shoulders, Adan picked oranges.

Swinging a hooked stick, he pulled down mangoes. He chopped breadfruit from a tall tree and dug out ñames. Finally, gripping a very long pole, he struck down coconuts.

"How do we get all the food down the mountain?" he asked.

"Watch," said Aunt Carmen. She whistled loudly.

Adan saw a patch of white moving in the trees. A horse with a golden mane appeared.

Uncle Ulise fed him a piece of fruit. The horse munched the delicious fruit loudly.

"Palomo will help us carry all the fruit and vegetables we've picked," Adan's mother said.

Back at the house, Adan gave Palomo another fruit.

"He'll go back up to the plantation now," his father said. "He's got all he wants to eat there."

Uncle Ulise rubbed his knee.

"What's the matter?" asked Adan's mother.

"My knee. It always hurts just before rain comes."

Adan looked at the cloudless sky. "But it's not going to rain."

"Yes, it will. My knee never lies. It'll rain tonight. Maybe tomorrow. Say! When it does, it'll be a yagua day!"

In the morning Adan, waking up cozy under his mosquito net, heard rain banging on the metal roof and tree frogs beeping like tiny car horns.

He jumped out of bed and got a big surprise. His mother and father, Uncle Ulise, and Aunt Carmen were on the porch wearing bathing suits.

"Let's go, Adan," his father said. "It's a wonderful yagua day. Put on your bathing suit!"

In the forest Adan heard shouts and swishing noises in the rain.

Racing into a clearing, he saw boys and girls shooting down a runway of grass, then disappearing over a ledge.

Uncle Ulise picked up a canoelike object from the grass. "This is a yagua, Adan. It fell from this palm tree."

"And this is what we do with it," said his
father. He ran, then belly-flopped on the
yagua. He skimmed down the grass, sailed up
into the air, and vanished over the ledge. His
mother did the same.

"Papi! Mami!"

Uncle Ulise laughed. "Don't worry, Adan.
They won't hurt themselves. The river is down
there. It makes a pool beneath the ledge. The
rain turns the grass butter-slick so you can zip
into the water. That's what makes it a yagua
day! Come and join us!"

That day Adan found out what fun a yagua
day is!

Two weeks later Adan moved a box of mangoes into his parents' store back in New York.

"Adan, my boy! Welcome home!" said Mail-carrier Jorge.

Adan smiled at Jorge. "You look sad, Jorge."

"Too much mail! Too much sun!"

"What you need is a yagua day."

"So you know what a yagua day is?"

"I had six yagua days in Puerto Rico."

"You went over the ledge?"

"Of course."

"Into the river?"

"*Si! Si!* Into the river. Sliding on yaguas!"

"Two-wheeled or four-wheeled yaguas?"

Adan laughed. "Yaguas don't have wheels. They come from palm trees."

"I thought they came from panel trucks like mine," teased Mailcarrier Jorge.

"Nothing grows in trucks, Jorge. These mangoes and oranges come from the trees. And the ñames come from under the ground. Wake up! Don't you know?"

Mailcarrier Jorge laughed. "Come, country boy, let's talk with your parents. I want to hear all about your visit to Corral Viejo!"

Comprehension Check

1. What is a yagua day?
2. At the beginning of the story, how did Adan feel about rainy weather? Why?
3. How did Mailcarrier Jorge and Adan's parents feel about rainy days? Why?
4. Do you think Adan is a helpful person? Why do you think as you do?
5. How did Adan feel when he saw his parents dressed in bathing suits on a rainy day?
6. What enjoyable things can you think of to do on a rainy day?

RAINING

by Rhoda W. Bacmeister

It's raining, raining, raining,
And all the world is wet.
It rained last night, and now today
It's raining, raining, yet!

Drip, drip, drip, drip,
Leaking from the eaves,
Pattering, splashing, and tapping
On the roof and the tulip tree's leaves.

194

The quick little raindrops in puddles
Are dancing up and down;
Rivers rush down the gutters,
Foamy and dirty brown.

Drip, drip, patter and splash,
How fast the raindrops race—
Running down the windowpane
Cold against my face!

The Baobab Automobile
by Jacqueline Held

Once upon a time there was a gentleman who
never cleaned his car. And the car was very
dirty.

The gentleman was particularly fond of dogs
too. As a matter of fact, he always kept his
dog, a basset, on the seat of his car. And
there was dog hair all over the car.

"Nothing to worry about," the gentleman-who-never-cleaned-his-car used to say. "Dogs are quite clean, you know. Dog hair is good for you."

Sometimes the gentleman would give some friends a ride in his car. And in winter those friends wore boots covered with mud.

"Please do get in and take a seat," said the gentleman-who-never-cleaned-his-car. And there was dog hair and mud all over the car.

"Nothing to worry about," the gentleman-who-never-cleaned-his-car used to say. "Mud baths are quite good for you."

Whenever the gentleman went swimming, he left his swimsuit to dry on the car seat. There was a lot of sand in the swimsuit. And there was dog hair and mud and sand all over the car.

"Nothing to worry about," the gentleman-who-never-cleaned-his-car used to say. "Sand is what you need to clean bumpers."

When the windows were down, the wind blew tiny seeds into the car. The seeds fell in the dog hair and mud and sand. And after a while something grew in the dog hair and mud and sand. It was crabgrass.

"Nothing to worry about," the gentleman-who-never-cleaned-his-car used to say. "Crab-grass makes me think of spring."

But there was something the gentleman did not know. Among the crabgrass seeds was a baobab seed.

The crabgrass grew. And the baobab grew. Then the crabgrass stopped growing. And the baobab went on growing.

Soon the baobab grew bigger than the gentleman's dog, the basset. And there was not much room left on the car seats.

"Nothing to worry about," the gentleman-who-never-cleaned-his-car used to say. "That is even better. My dog will be in the shade."

On and on grew the baobab. One day it was as
big as a cherry tree. This was the same day that
the gentleman cut a hole in the roof of his car.

"Nothing to worry about," the gentleman-who-
never-cleaned-his-car used to say. "That is even
more fun. How strange, really. I would never
have thought of buying a car with an open top!"

The baobab grew through the car roof. On and
on it grew.

The basset found all this very exciting. It
had always been sad because it was so close to
the ground. So the basset climbed up the baobab.
And there it built a hut.

"How strange, really," the small basset used
to say. "How beautiful the world is when you
see it from above. I would never have thought
that it made things look so different!"

I think that the car is still running about,
with the gentleman, the basset, the sand, the
mud, the seeds, the crabgrass—and the baobab, of
course.

Perhaps someday, as you are going downtown,
you'll meet the baobab automobile. And you'll
know it at once.

The basset is still at the top of the baobab
where it can see far and wide. It barks out
directions to the gentleman. "Bus on the left
side! Truck on the right side!"

The gentleman has never had an accident. He
feels quite safe in his baobab automobile.

Comprehension Check

1. How did the gentleman get dog hair, mud, and sand in his car?
2. How did the gentleman feel about his dirty car?
3. What two kinds of seeds blew in the window?
4. Do you think the gentleman was happy with the baobab automobile? Explain why you think as you do.
5. What would you do if a big tree grew in your living room?

You just read about a baobab tree growing in an automobile. You might have thought there wasn't such a tree. But there really is. It's an unusual tree. You'll find out just how unusual as you read this selection.

The Pumpkin Tree

by Ryerson Johnson

What if your class were on a nature walk and it started to rain? Where could you go to stay dry? If you lived in some places in Africa or Australia, you might go inside a fat old baobab tree. That's right. Not *under* a baobab tree. *Inside* of it!

The baobab tree looks a little like a giant pumpkin, but it is not yellow or orange. It's almost as wide as it is tall. It has short branches sticking out from the top of the pumpkin part. There would be plenty of room inside the trunk for you and all your friends.

How would you like to live inside a tree? How would you like to sleep, get up in the morning, and eat breakfast there? The wood inside a baobab tree is not very hard. It's so soft that sometimes people hollow it out to make a house. This doesn't seem to hurt the tree. It just keeps right on growing. Sometimes it grows for another thousand years! It lives longer than almost anything in the world.

If you get hungry while you are in the tree, you can cook the leaves and eat them. And the tree has a fruit that some people say tastes like gingerbread. So, instead of a pumpkin tree, maybe you'd rather call the baobab a gingerbread tree.

If you had a pet elephant and wanted to tie it up, you could make a very strong rope from the baobab bark. And if your pet got hungry, you could feed it some of the tree. But you would have to be careful about this. Elephants like the baobab so much that sometimes they eat the whole tree—trunk, branches, leaves, and all!

Comprehension Check

1. Where do baobab trees grow?
2. What is the inside of a baobab tree like?
3. How long does a baobab tree live?
4. What does the fruit of the baobab tree taste like?
5. Would the baobab tree make a good club house? Tell why you think as you do.
6. What would you do if you had a baobab tree in your backyard?

Skill Check

Read each sentence below. Tell whether the sentence is fact or fiction.

1. A baobab tree lives longer than almost anything in the world.
2. The baobab tree grew through the car roof.
3. The baobab tree has a fruit that some people say tastes like gingerbread.
4. The basset built a hut in the baobab tree.
5. The baobab tree is almost as wide as it is tall.

Recognizing Realistic and Fanciful Stories

Skill Lesson

Most stories that you read are made-up stories. A story or paragraph is <u>realistic</u> if it tells about something that could really happen. A <u>fanciful</u> story or paragraph is one that tells about something that could never really happen.

Read the two paragraphs that follow.

It was a great day for the parade. Felix watched as the band marched down the street. The music made him clap his hands and stamp his feet. Giant balloons floated high in the air. The clowns made everyone laugh. This was the best parade Felix had ever seen.

The wizard touched Jenny with his magic
stick and told her that she could fly.
Jenny jumped off the ground and started
waving her arms. "Whoopee!" she shouted.
"I think I'll fly across town to visit my
grandmother."

Which of the two paragraphs is realistic? Why?
Which paragraph is fanciful? Why?

206

Practice

Read the two paragraphs below. Tell why you think one paragraph is realistic. Tell why you think one paragraph is fanciful.

The elephants were looking for food in the jungle. Soon they found the kind of trees they liked. With their trunks they pulled leaves from the trees and ate them. Some monkeys who lived in the trees were angry. The elephants were eating their home!

Sandra was a special girl who lived under the sea. Her friends were the animals that lived under the sea too. She played tag with an octopus and jumped rope with sea horses. When she was tired, she went to sleep in a bed of sea flowers.

As you read the next story, "Why Cowboys Sing, in Texas," decide if it is realistic or fanciful.

Why Cowboys Sing, in Texas

by Le Grand

Today, cowboys sing, in Texas. They sing "Yippee yi, yippee yay." Everybody knows how cowboys sing, today, in Texas.

But it was not always so. Things were quiet, once, in Texas. Long ago, cowboys were silent. And the most silent cowboy in all of Texas was Slim Jim Bean.

Once, in that old and silent time, Slim Jim was guarding a herd of cattle at night.

It was a long, dark night. And Slim Jim Bean was lonely.

"I wish I could hear a little noise," he thought. "Any kind of a little noise that would not frighten the cows."

208

Slim Jim knew that if anything frightened the cows, they would stampede. They would stampede and run all over Texas.

Slim Jim thought of just the noise he would like to hear. It was a song he sang when he was a boy. He remembered the words and the tune.

"I believe I could sing that song again," he said. "A little song should not frighten the cows."

So Slim Jim opened his mouth and he sang.

The song woke the cows. And they didn't like it. They couldn't stand the song.

A big black cow stampeded.

A little yellow cow stampeded.

Big ones and little ones, spotted ones and plain ones—they all stampeded. They stampeded all over Texas.

Slim Jim and the other cowboys rode out to round up the cows.

They rode through the mesquite with its long, straight thorns.

They rode through the Spanish dagger with its long, sharp spikes.

They rode through the cat's-claw with its long, curved briers.

And they rode through clumps of cactus with its long, prickly needles.

But the thorns did not hurt them. And the spikes did not hurt them. And the briers did not hurt them. And the needles did not hurt them, because the cowboys wore leather chaps on their legs.

Slim Jim was the best rider and the best roper in all Texas. But it took him and the other cowboys half a month of Sundays to round up those cows.

"Now, listen!" the other cowboys said to
Slim Jim. "No more singing in Texas."

Slim Jim promised he would sing no more.
He would sing no more, in Texas.

That night Slim Jim went out to guard the
cows again.

It was very quiet, and Slim Jim was lonely.
He thought about his song. The song kept running
through his mind.

Slim Jim tried to keep his promise. He
tried hard not to sing. But the song went round
and round in his mind. It went round and round.

Slim Jim couldn't hold it back. He opened
his mouth and he sang his song.

And the cows didn't like it.

A little tan cow stampeded.

A big red cow stampeded.

Big ones and little ones, spotted ones and
plain ones—they all stampeded. They stampeded
all over Texas.

Slim Jim and the other cowboys had to ride through all those thorny bushes again.

This time it took them nearly a whole month of Sundays to round up these cows.

"Now, listen!" the other cowboys said to Slim Jim. "There will be no more singing. No more singing in Texas."

"I can't promise," Slim Jim said. "It's lonely at night on this lone prairie. That song keeps running through my mind. It goes round and round. And when that happens, I have to sing it."

Then Slim Jim got on his horse and said, "I can't promise not to sing. So I will go away. I will go far away. I will find a place where there are no cows to be frightened by my singing." And Slim Jim rode away.

On the tenth day Slim Jim came to a river.
It was a very dry river. It was so dry that it
was dusty. So Slim Jim knew it was the Rio
Grande. Everyone in Texas knows the Rio Grande
is the dustiest river in the world.

There was a little water out in the middle.
But not enough for the fish to swim in. They
had to walk on the bottom.

Slim Jim could see them walking around
down there.

"Hmm," he said, "a tasty fish would make a
fine supper."

Slim Jim was a cowboy, not a fisherman. He
had no fishhooks and he had no fishline.

But Slim Jim saw that there was only enough river to cover the smallest fish. The biggest ones were half out of water as they walked along the bottom.

Slim Jim was a cowboy, and he was a good roper. He was the best roper in all Texas. So he whirled his rope—and he roped a fish.

Slim Jim camped on the riverbank and cooked his fish.

It was lonely there, beside the river. Slim Jim's song kept running through his mind. He opened his mouth and he sang. He sang that song. And his song did not frighten the fish in the Rio Grande. Not a single fish stampeded.

"This is the place for me," Slim Jim said. "I shall stay here, and sing, and fish."

So Slim Jim laid aside his leather cowboy chaps, because he would not need them. And he stayed beside the river. And he fished. And he sang.

214

But while Slim Jim fished and sang there was trouble in Texas.

The other cowboys remembered Slim Jim's song. That song kept running through their minds. It went round and round.

They just couldn't help it—they sang that song.

And the cows didn't like it. They couldn't stand that song.

A big brown cow stampeded.

A little white cow stampeded.

Big ones and little ones, spotted ones and plain ones—they all stampeded. They stampeded all over Texas.

The cowboys rode for a month of Sundays. They couldn't get the cows rounded up again.

Then up spoke a cowboy of the Pecos country.

"We need help," he said. "Slim Jim Bean is the best cowboy in all Texas. We must get Slim Jim to help us round up those cows."

The other cowboys agreed.

So they rode out to find Slim Jim.

They rode all over Texas. They rode until they came to the Rio Grande.

And that was where they found Slim Jim, fishing.

"Cows are stampeding all over Texas, Slim Jim," they told him. "We must get them rounded up again or Texas will be ruined. You must help us round up those cows, Slim Jim."

Slim Jim turned away from the river.

His voice rose loud and free.

"Slim Jim will ride and round them up," he cried. "All you cowboys follow me."

So Slim Jim rode to round up the cows.

He rode through all those thorny bushes.

And Slim Jim felt the thorns. He felt them because he was not wearing his leather chaps.

When he felt the mesquite thorns, Slim Jim shouted, "Yip!"

When he felt the Spanish dagger spikes, Slim Jim shouted, "Yippee!"

When he felt the cat's-claw briers, Slim Jim shouted, "Yi!"

When he felt the cactus needles, Slim Jim shouted, "Yay!"

And when he felt them all at the same time, Slim Jim shouted, "Yippee yi, yippee yay!"

Slim Jim rode through all the thorny bushes in Texas. And his voice rose loud and free, "Yippee yi, yippee yay!"

Everywhere that Slim Jim rode, the cows heard him. The cows that were stampeding all over Texas heard him. They liked those new sounds that Slim Jim made. They stopped running to listen to Slim Jim's yips, yippees, yis, and yays.

The other cowboys said, "Make those noises again, Slim Jim. The noises the cows like."

So Slim Jim made the noises again. Then he made a song out of those noises.

Yippee yi, yippee yay-yippee.

218

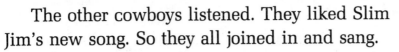

The other cowboys listened. They liked Slim Jim's new song. So they all joined in and sang.

The cows liked the new song.

The big cows liked it.

The little cows liked it.

Big ones and little ones, spotted ones and plain ones—they all stopped to listen.

Then Slim Jim and the other cowboys rounded them up.

And that was the end of the big stampede, in Texas.

And that is why cowboys sing, today, in Texas.

They sing, "Yippee yi, yippee yay."

They sing Slim Jim's song, today, in Texas.

Comprehension Check

1. What did Slim Jim decide to do when he couldn't help singing? What did he decide to do instead of watching cows?
2. Why did Slim Jim cry out, "Yip, yippee, yi, yay!" when he was rounding up the cows?
3. What kind of person do you think Slim Jim Bean was? Tell why you think as you do.
4. Whose song do cowboys sing in Texas?
5. Why do cowboys sing the song?
6. Think of a song you know. Make up a story that tells how the song began.

Skill Check

Read the sentences below. Which sentences are realistic? Which sentences are fanciful? Tell why.

1. Slim Jim opened his mouth and sang.
2. The fish walked on the bottom of the river.
3. Slim Jim and other cowboys rode out to round up the cows.
4. Slim Jim whirled his rope and roped a fish.
5. Slim Jim was lonely.

The Queen Who Changed Places with the King

by Nancy West

The queen dropped her sewing to the floor. "I am tired," she said, "of doing fancy sewing. I'm tired of baking tarts and playing a game of bridge now and then. I am tired of sitting quietly at home here in the castle. I am tired and unhappy. I want to get out and do things."

The king sighed. "I am tired," he said. "As soon as I slay one dragon, there's another one I must go out and slay. You don't know how lucky you are. You don't have to go out and slay dragons every day."

"I am just as tired of what I do as you are of what you do," said the queen.

"I would give anything," said the king, "if I could sit here quietly. I'd like to bake tarts and play a game of bridge now and then."

"Well, I would like to be out in the fresh air," said the queen. "I would carry a sword and look for dragons to slay. That would put some excitement into my life."

"And staying home would put some peace into my life," said the king.

"Let's try it," said the queen.

"I will if you will," said the king.

222

So the king stayed home the next day. The queen got on a shiny black horse and rode off to preview Dragon Country. She wanted to look around before she started slaying dragons. "At last," she said, "I'm out of the house."

The queen went on until she came to the Forest of the Dragons. There were caves everywhere. Some had white marks in front of them. Some had laundry hanging out to dry.

The queen saw a young dragon that was about eight years old. "Why do some caves have white marks," she asked, "and some have laundry?"

"The marks on the caves show where the king has slain dragons," said the young dragon. "The laundry at the caves shows where dragons still live. They wash things and hang them out to dry."

The queen took the sword from her belt and
rode from cave to cave, looking in. The dragons
looked back at her with frightened eyes.

The queen got down from her horse. She let
the sword fall to the ground. "I won't do it,"
she said. "I just don't want to slay a dragon."

She remounted her horse and rode back through
the woods. The dragons waved to her.

Back at the castle, the queen found the king sitting with bandages on his fingers. He was trying to unknot some thread.

"Fancy sewing is not as easy as it looks," he said. "The thread keeps getting knotted. And I have stuck my fingers about a hundred times. I don't like baking tarts either. I always forget to preheat the oven. Why must I do this just because queens have always done it?"

"There is something I must tell you," the queen said.

"I suppose you don't want to go out and slay dragons anymore," said the king.

"That's right, I don't. I just don't know why people slay dragons," said the queen.

"Because they have always slain dragons, that's why," said the king.

"That's not a good enough reason for me,"
the queen said. She took his hands and looked
at the bandages. "It's just like fancy sewing
and baking tarts. Why should queens do those
things just because queens have always done
them? And why should kings slay dragons just
because kings have always done it?"

"Well," the king said, "why indeed? I think
we should replant the old vegetable garden."

So the king and the queen grew beets and
carrots and tomatoes.

There were no more marks outside the caves in the Forest of the Dragons. Only laundry.

And every other Sunday the king and queen invited the dragon families to the castle.

They had tea and played a game of bridge now and then.

228

Comprehension Check

1. How did the queen and the king feel about their lives?
2. What was the first thing they did to change their lives?
3. Why didn't the queen want to slay dragons after she visited their caves?
4. What kind of person was the queen? Tell why you think as you do.
5. Do you think the queen and king were happy after they decided to grow vegetables? Why or why not?

Skill Check

Read each sentence below. Find the prefix and root word in the underlined words. Then select the correct answer to each question.

1. I always forget to preheat the oven.
   What does preheat mean?
   a. heat again   b. heat before
2. The queen was unhappy with her life.
   What does unhappy mean?
   a. not happy   b. very happy
3. The queen remounted her horse.
   What does remounted mean?
   a. not mounted   b. mounted again
4. The king was trying to unknot some thread.
   What does unknot mean?
   a. knot   b. take the knot out

Petey

by Tobi Tobias

In the afternoon, like always, when I get
home from school and say hello to Mom and check
out what Benjy, my little brother, is up to and
grab an apple, then I run upstairs and I drop
my school bag on my bed and see what my silly
old gerbil, Petey, is doing. Usually he's
banging this tin juice can he's so crazy about
against the glass sides of his cage, making a
whole song of happy clinks and clunks. He does
it at night too, and Daddy always says, when
he comes in to kiss me, "How can you go to sleep
with that racket?" but the real truth is I can
hardly go to sleep without it. It's a friendly noise.

Or maybe he's building a fancy new nest for himself out of the cedar shavings and shredded burlap I put there for him. Or running himself dizzy in his exercise wheel. Or prying open a sunflower seed with his little paws and his tiny sharp teeth, or washing his funny mouse face or grooming his funny mouse tail. And then when he hears me (he really knows the sound of my voice), he stops what he's doing, sits up on his hind paws, looks around with his bright brown eyes, and I put my hand into the cage and he whisks right into it.

But this afternoon I get home late because it's my ice-skating day. It's beginning to get dark in my room, and I can hardly see him. But then I do. He's all huddled up in a corner of his cage like he's shivering, and when I call out, "Petey, I'm home. Want a piece of apple? Want a sunflower seed?" he doesn't sit up, and right away I know something bad is going to happen.

I call Daddy. That's how it is with me. For the everyday things I call Mommy. Sometimes she says I call her a hundred times a day. And for the one or two really scary things I call Daddy. And he comes and looks, and I can tell by his face what he's thinking is what I'm thinking too.

"Petey's sick, Emily," he says. And then comes the worst part. Very slowly, Daddy says, "You know, honey, Petey's almost five years old now and that's getting to be pretty old for a gerbil—"

"No," I say. Just "No."

"OK, Em," Daddy says. "Let's see what we can do for him."

So we look in the *How to Care for Your Pets* book we have, and it does not tell us any good news. "You can't really doctor a gerbil," it says, "you pretty much have to wait and see what happens. If you have a sick gerbil one night," it says, "it's likely the next morning you'll

either have a well gerbil or a dead gerbil." All
I can say is the people who wrote that book must
never have had a gerbil they loved or they
wouldn't talk so smart.

Well, even if the book says there is nothing
you can do, we do everything we can think of.
We change Petey's water, getting it just right between warm and cold, and we add a few drops of
hamster medicine to it and try to coax Petey to
drink. But he won't. Or maybe he can't. So
we try plain water, because we think maybe he
doesn't like the smell of the medicine, but
Petey doesn't want that either. Then we shell
some sunflower seeds and mash up the soft
insides. I put the mash on my fingertip so Petey
can lick it off. But he doesn't.

All the time we're doing this, Daddy is talking to me.

"Look at it this way, Em. Petey may be a well gerbil. The book says so. There's as much chance of that as—anything else."

"You were the one who said he was getting old," I yell, getting mad at him because I feel so terrible about Petey and not being able to do anything to help.

"Four or five years is a long life for a gerbil, Emmy. We've got to face up to that."

"It doesn't seem long to me," I say.

"Honey, think what a great time he's had with you. You've taken such good care of him. I don't just mean the feeding and keeping his cage clean. I mean all the talking and playing and loving."

Petey still won't take the food, and there is a long silence between the three of us.

After a while Daddy says, "Em, if someone's going to die, it's better this way. It really is. Sometimes when animals or people get old, their sickness comes on slowly, and it can be a very long time of hurting for them and everyone who loves them."

"Let's just be quiet," I say. "Maybe Petey's trying to sleep." But both of us know that Petey never needed quiet for sleeping. Just the way I could sleep with his racket he could sleep with mine.

After supper Daddy and I are watching over Petey again, and Benjy comes in. "Here," he says, and he gives me a little piece off his sucking blanket. "For Petey." I fold it up like a little pillow and put it under Petey's head. Benjy is scared. "Is Petey going to die?" he asks Daddy.

"I'm afraid he is, Ben," Daddy says, "but we're still hoping he won't."

When I wake up in the middle of that night, it's still the same with Petey. I try the food and the water again, but he doesn't care. Then I try just sitting by his cage and stroking his soft, shiny fur with my finger. Even if it doesn't help, maybe he knows I'm there, and anyway I know I'm there, and that makes me feel a little better. After a while it gets cold sitting on the floor by Petey's cage, so I get back into my bed and pull up the covers the way Petey burrows into his nest of soft burlap and good-smelling shavings, and I think about how cute he was when he was a little baby, and I guess I finally fall asleep.

236

In the morning, right when I wake up, I don't remember for a minute, but then I do, and it hits me like someone threw a rock at my stomach. I go over to Petey's cage, very quietly. He's stretched out by his exercise wheel, not moving. I try to call Mommy and Daddy, but I haven't any voice left. I guess they know I need someone, though, and they come into my room. I forget which one of us says, "He's dead," but anyway I'm crying while Mommy holds me tight. I think she's crying a little too.

Then, all of a sudden, we start to talk
about all the things we remember about him,
all his little ways and tricks, and how smart
and beautiful he was. We're telling each other
the crazy adventures he's had, like the time
he knocked the screen lid off his cage and ran
away. We chased after him, but that must have
scared him, and he wouldn't come out, and we
couldn't find him anywhere. We finally found him
on a shelf in the kitchen, curled up in a box of
oatmeal, sleepy and full, with a funny look on
his face, like he was laughing.

Then we have breakfast.

Afterward Mommy gets her best box—the one her silver birthday bracelet came in—and we put some colored tissue paper in it, and then she puts Petey in, very gently. We all give him good-by pats, even Benjy, who's a little scared to.

We bury him in the backyard, just under where the shadow of the swing falls when it's swinging the highest.

I miss him. Every time I look at the empty cage I feel empty inside me. I miss him when Benjy finds a box of sunflower seeds and starts shelling them and eating the juicy insides. I miss him when Mommy scoops the frozen orange juice out of the tin can. I miss him when I see anything soft and shreddy that would be good to make a nest with. It's like things are all over the place, reminding me. Whenever I think about Petey, I love remembering all the good times we had, but then I feel awful because there won't be any more. Mostly I miss him when I'm going to sleep. It's so quiet.

240

It's starting to be spring now. I'm coming home from skating again, and Mommy's on the telephone. She says, "I'll ask her, Helen, and I'll let you know. Thanks a lot," and hangs up.

She says, "Hi," and "Don't put those wet skates on the table," and gives me a kiss. I give her a wet apple kiss back. She says, "That was Helen," and she tells me that our friends Helen and George's two gerbils that they thought were brothers just had a litter of five babies, so one of them isn't. I laugh, and then I feel sad, because I think of Petey. Mommy says Helen and George know how bad I feel that Petey died, and they'd like to give me two of the babies when they're old enough to leave their mother.

I test out the idea in my head, but it doesn't feel too good. No one, no one could be like Petey. I say, "Not right now."

Mommy says, "No, not right now. But in a while."

I say, "It won't be the same."

Mommy says, "I never said it would be the same. It can be different, Em, and still be good."

I'm going to think it over and let her know.

Comprehension Check

1. What kind of things did Petey do when he was not sleeping?
2. How did Petey act when he became sick?
3. What did the book *How to Care for Your Pets* say about sick gerbils?
4. How did Emily feel when Petey died? How did her family help her?
5. Do you think Emily will take the two gerbils that her mother's friends offered her? Why do you think as you do?
6. Suppose you had a sick pet. What would you do?

Literary Unit

The Hairy Dog

by Herbert Asquith

My dog's so furry I've not seen
His face for years and years:
His eyes are buried out of sight,
I only guess his ears.

When people ask me for his breed,
I do not know or care:
He has the beauty of them all
Hidden beneath his hair.

Comparing Things That Are Different

Two things can be different and alike at the same time. Do you know how? Read the paragraph about the elephant and the paragraph about the frog. Then talk about the ways in which the two animals are alike and different.

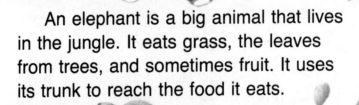

An elephant is a big animal that lives in the jungle. It eats grass, the leaves from trees, and sometimes fruit. It uses its trunk to reach the food it eats.

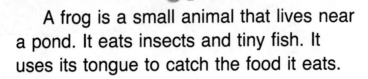

A frog is a small animal that lives near a pond. It eats insects and tiny fish. It uses its tongue to catch the food it eats.

244

The elephant and the frog are two very different animals. However, they are alike in some ways too. Each one is a certain size, each one lives someplace, each one eats certain foods, and each one catches or grabs its food in some way.

The sentences below can help you compare how an elephant and a frog are alike.

1. Big is to elephant as _____ is to frog.
2. Jungle is to elephant as _____ is to frog.
3. Leaves and grass are to elephant as _____ and _____ are to frog.

Practice

Read the two paragraphs that follow. Then compare the penguin and the flamingo in the questions that follow the paragraphs.

The penguin is a bird that lays eggs and builds a nest. It has black and white feathers and a small, sharp beak. It lives in places where the weather is cold. It sees ice and snow all the time. The penguin does not fly. Its wings are too small. However, it is a good swimmer.

The flamingo is also a bird that lays eggs and builds a nest. It has pink feathers and a large beak. It lives in warm places. It sees grass and trees all the time. The flamingo does not swim. However, it is a very good flier.

Answer the two questions, then complete the sentence.

1. Where do penguins live?
2. Where do flamingos live?
3. Warm weather is to the flamingo as _____ weather is to the penguin.

Answer the two questions, then complete the sentence.

1. How do flamingos get from place to place?
2. How do penguins get from place to place?
3. Flying is to the flamingo as _____ is to the penguin.

In the next story, "An Anteater Named Arthur," you will find examples where two different things are compared. Think about the ways in which the two things are alike and different.

An Anteater Named Arthur

by Bernard Waber

Let me tell you about Arthur.

First, I will tell you what Arthur is like
most of the time. Most of the time, Arthur is
a kind, helpful, understanding, well-behaved,
sensible, orderly, responsible, loving, lovable,
altogether wonderful son.

But . . .
sometimes Arthur is a problem; not all of
the time, mind you, just sometimes.
I will explain.

Sometimes Arthur doesn't understand.

"I don't understand," says Arthur.
"What don't you understand?" I ask.

"We are called anteaters, right?"
"Right," I answer.
"Why must we be called by what we eat?"
"Because it happens that we are," I tell him.

"A cat eats fish, right?" Arthur asks.
"Right," I answer.
"A bird eats worms, right?"
"Right."
"A cow eats grass, right?"
"Right," I answer again.

"But the cat is not called a fisheater,
the bird is not called a wormeater,
and the cow is not called a grasseater.
Right?" Arthur asks.
"Right," I answer.

"Then I shall be called by another name."
"What will you be called?" I ask.

"I shall be called a 'blion.'"
"But you are not a 'blion,'" I tell him.
"Then I shall be called a 'swhale.'"
"But you are not a 'swhale.'"
"Then I shall be called a 'melephant.'"
"But you are not a 'melephant.'"
"Then I shall be called a 'brabbit.'"
"But you are not a 'brabbit.'"
"What shall I be called?" Arthur asks.

"You shall be called an anteater," I tell him.
"An anteater named Arthur."

Sometimes Arthur is choosy.

"Breakfast! Breakfast is ready!"
I call to Arthur.

Arthur comes down.
"What are we having?" he asks.
"We are having ants," I answer.

"What kind of ants?"
"The red ones," I tell him.
Arthur makes a face.
I pretend not to notice.

"Look at them," I say in my cheeriest voice.
"Aren't these the most beautiful ants you
have ever seen . . . in all your life?
I gathered them especially for you."
Arthur looks and makes another face.
"Arthur," I go on, "red ants are delicious;
and so good for you too. Don't you want
to grow up to be big and strong?"
More faces from Arthur.

"I have an idea," I say, "how about if I
sprinkle sugar on them? Red ants are simply
delicious with sugar."
Arthur shakes his head.
"A twist of lemon, perhaps?"
More head shaking from Arthur.
"Arthur, red ants aren't exactly easy to come
by!" I remind him. "You have to scratch mighty
deep for red ants!"
Arthur begins playing with his spoon.

"You ought to at least try one," I continue.
"You will never know if you like something
unless you give it a chance. Here, how about
this one?"

"Ilk!" says Arthur, turning his head away.

"Very well!" I exclaim at last. "Never mind
about the red ants. Never mind that you are
missing out on the world's tastiest, most
delicious, most scrumptious dish. What will
you eat instead?"

"Brown ants," Arthur answers.

254

Sometimes Arthur forgets.

"Good-by," says Arthur,
rushing off to school.
"Good-by," I say.
The door closes.

The door opens.
"What did you forget?" I ask.
"I forgot my spelling book,"
he answers.

Up he runs,
two steps at a time.

Down he comes with
his spelling book.

"Good-by," says Arthur.
"Good-by," I say.
The door closes.

The door opens.

"What did you forget?" I ask.

"I forgot my sneakers," he answers.

Up he runs, two steps at a time.

Down he comes with his sneakers.

"Good-by," says Arthur.

"Good-by," I say.

The door closes.

The door opens.

"What did you forget?" I ask.

"I forgot my pencil case,"
he answers.

Up he runs,
two steps at a time.

Down he comes with
his pencil case.

"Arthur," I say to him, "you will have to try
to remember not to forget. Now stop and think.
Do you have everything you need?"
"Yes," Arthur answers.
"You are absolutely, positively, without a
shade of a doubt, one hundred percent sure now?"
"Yes, I am absolutely, positively, without a
shade of a doubt, one hundred percent sure,"
he answers.

"Good-by then."
"Good-by," says Arthur.
The door closes.
I will wait to see if it will open again.

I am not disappointed.
The door opens.
"What did you forget?" I ask.
"I forgot to kiss you good-by," he answers.

"Good-by," says Arthur.
"Good-by," I say.
The door closes.

See what I mean about Arthur?

Skills Unit 13

Comprehension Check

1. What is Arthur like most of the time?
2. What kinds of problems does Arthur's mother have with him?
3. Does Arthur have a good reason to want to change his name? Tell why or why not.
4. Make up another part to the story. Tell about a funny problem Arthur might have.

Skill Check

Answer the first two questions. Then tell what words finish the last three sentences.

1. Why is an anteater called an anteater?
2. How would you rename these animals to tell what they eat?

> cow   bird   cat

Use the word that tells what each animal eats.

3. Ant is to anteater as _____ is to cow.
4. Ant is to anteater as _____ is to bird.
5. Ant is to anteater as _____ is to cat.

What's a Ghost Going to Do?

by Jane Thayer

Gussie was a friendly ghost, who lived in an attic apartment in an old house in the country. The house was so old that its shingles curled, its windows were cracked, and its paint was peeling.

In the summer Mr. and Mrs. Scott and Susie and Sammy Scott lived in the house. The Scotts didn't believe in ghosts, but when Gussie banged and clanked with her bang-clank equipment, they told their friends proudly, "We've got a ghost named Gussie."

When the Scotts moved out in the fall, Mouse moved in. Gussie made cheesecake for him, and they played checkers by a crackling log fire. Summer and winter, Gussie led a happy life.

One day, when the birds had flown south and the Scotts would be leaving soon, Gussie was hanging around when she heard Mr. Scott talking to Mrs. Scott.

"I think I'll sell the house to the government," Mr. Scott said. "The government is buying old houses and tearing them down to make a park here. They will tear this one down."

"Then we can build a new house," Mrs. Scott said.

Gussie was shocked. "Tear the house down?" she thought. It was the only home she had ever known. Where would she go if they tore it down? "Oh, I've got to put some thoughts in Mr. Scott's head," she decided. So she followed Mr. Scott around the house, trying to put some thoughts in his head.

"This is a lovely old house!" cried Gussie in ghostly language.

Mr. Scott wasn't listening.

She followed Mr. Scott around the garden. "There aren't many like it left!" cried Gussie in ghostly language.

Mr. Scott wasn't listening.

"Don't sell it!" begged Gussie.

Still Mr. Scott didn't hear. Gussie climbed back to her attic apartment, groaning with despair. She couldn't go with the Scotts. Ghosts never live in *new* houses. What was she going to do?

The Scotts sold the house. They began to clear everything out. They held a sale, and people came to buy the furniture and dishes.

Gussie wandered about as things were carried out, wailing and wringing her hands. The house was empty now. The Scotts closed the door for the last time.

"Good-by, house," they said rather sadly. "Good-by, Gussie."

"Don't go!" cried Gussie in anguish from the window of her attic apartment.

But the Scotts went off. Gussie waved her handkerchief, ghostly tears streaming down her face until the car was lost from sight.

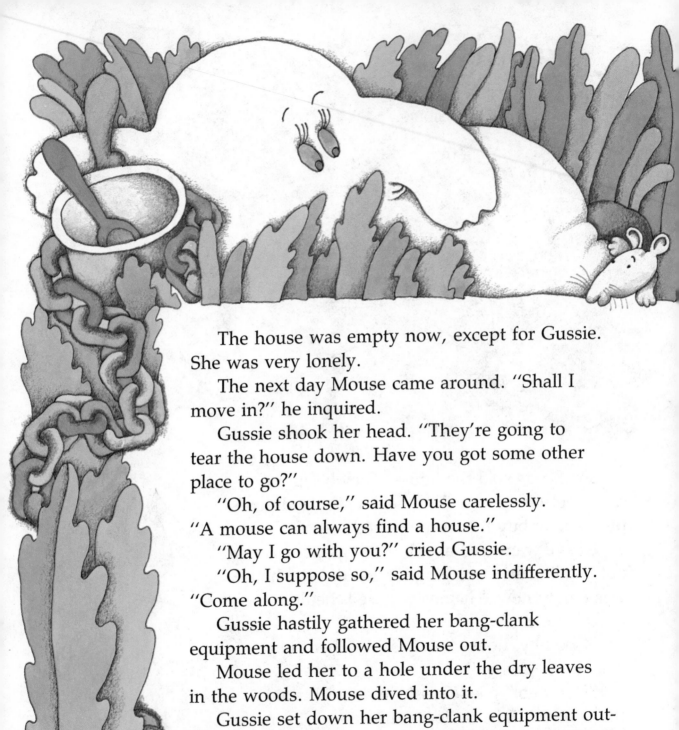

The house was empty now, except for Gussie. She was very lonely.

The next day Mouse came around. "Shall I move in?" he inquired.

Gussie shook her head. "They're going to tear the house down. Have you got some other place to go?"

"Oh, of course," said Mouse carelessly. "A mouse can always find a house."

"May I go with you?" cried Gussie.

"Oh, I suppose so," said Mouse indifferently. "Come along."

Gussie hastily gathered her bang-clank equipment and followed Mouse out.

Mouse led her to a hole under the dry leaves in the woods. Mouse dived into it.

Gussie set down her bang-clank equipment outside the door. She began to squeeze through the hole. Even though she was a ghostly ghost and held her breath, it was a terribly tight fit.

264

Mouse popped impatiently out of another hole.

"Don't take all day," he said crossly.

"Help me!" gasped Gussie.

Mouse popped into the hole again and grabbed Gussie's legs. Gussie wiggled, Mouse pulled, and at last Gussie found herself, a little black and blue, down in Mouse's house.

"You're going to crowd me," complained Mouse.

Gussie made herself as small as she could. She didn't want to be any bother. But she soon saw, from Mouse's muttering and stamping about, that she was in the way. She was quite uncomfortable, too, in such cramped quarters. In the night she heard rain pounding on Mouse's house.

"Oh, my bang-clank equipment will rust," she thought in dismay.

"May I bring my bang-clank equipment in out of the rain?" she asked.

"No, you may not," said Mouse.

Gussie sat crunched in a corner all night.
As soon as daylight came she got up painfully
and wiggled her way back through the hole. Sure
enough, her precious bang-clank equipment was
red with rust.

"Thanks just the same, Mouse," called Gussie
down the hole. "I am going home. I'll stay till
they tear the house down."

She lugged her bang-clank equipment home and
spent the day removing the rust.

266

Once more she put her mind on the problem
of where to live. "I'll advertise," she thought.
She put an ad in the newspaper:

Ghost, named Gussie,
experienced, friendly, needs a good home.

She looked in the mailbox every day, but no
reply came. No one wanted to give a ghost a
home.

Then a government man, Mr. McGovern, came round to see if the house was empty, so he could tear it down.

When Gussie heard his key in the lock she thought, "Oh, perhaps I have one last chance!"

She hurried downstairs. She followed as Mr. McGovern walked from room to room. "This is a lovely old house!" cried Gussie in loud ghostly language.

Mr. McGovern wasn't listening.

"There aren't many like it left!" cried Gussie in louder ghostly language. Mr. McGovern wasn't listening.

"What's a ghost going to do? Don't tear it down!" cried Gussie, and in her despair she hammered Mr. McGovern on the head.

All Mr. McGovern seemed to feel was a light breeze on his bald head. But suddenly he stood still.

"I've just had an idea!" he exclaimed. Gussie stood still too.

"This is a lovely old house. There aren't many like it left," Mr. McGovern said.

Gussie held her breath.

"I won't tear it down!" cried Mr. McGovern. "We'll use it for a museum in the park!"

Gussie almost fainted with joy.

The government man got busy at once on his wonderful idea.

He called in carpenters and painters. They took off the old curling roof and nailed on new shingles. They repaired the window glass and put on fresh white paint. Gussie was everywhere, she was so thrilled.

Mr. McGovern brought in handsome old grand-father clocks, spinning wheels, trundle beds, brass candlesticks, and all sorts of ancient relics. Gussie ran her fingers lovingly over the old things. Mr. McGovern put up a sign: **MUSEUM.** He stood outside, admiring the place. Gussie stood behind him.

"That was a splendid idea of mine," Mr. McGovern said.

"All it needs is a ghost," said Gussie.

"All it needs is a ghost," said Mr. McGovern. "Where did I see something about a ghost? I know, in the newspaper."

He pulled the newspaper out of his pocket and there was the ad:

Ghost, named Gussie,
experienced, friendly, needs a good home.

"Answer it," said Gussie, who wanted to know that she was welcome in the museum.

"I'll answer it," Mr. McGovern said. He mailed a letter to Gussie.

Dear Gussie,

You are cordially invited to make your home in the new Park Museum.

Sincerely,
Mr. McGovern

"How will we know if she accepts?" Mr. McGovern wondered.

"Bang! Clank!" said Gussie.

"Good!" said Mr. McGovern.

Then people poured in to see all the ancient relics in the Park Museum. Mr. McGovern explained about hoopskirts and warming pans. He told them to notice the lovely old house, for there weren't many like it left.

Gussie looked after everything. She banged and clanked.

"And we've got a ghost!" said Mr. McGovern proudly.

Comprehension Check

1. Why did the Scotts sell their house?
2. How did Gussie feel about the Scotts' moving away? Why?
3. Who offered Gussie a home? Was she happy in her new home? Why or why not?
4. What did Mr. McGovern decide to do about the old house? How did Gussie help him decide?
5. What are some other things an empty old house might become?

Skill Check

1. What was Gussie's problem?
2. How did Gussie solve her problem?
3. Do you think Gussie's solution was a good one? Why or why not?

Using Figures of Speech to Compare Things

A **figure of speech** is a colorful way to compare two things. A figure of speech often makes reading more interesting and helps the reader get a better understanding of what is described.

Rosalie took her brother Quentin to see his first circus. "The bareback rider was as beautiful as a fairy princess," Rosalie said later. "Her dress looked like stars in the sky."

Rosalie used two figures of speech. She compared the bareback rider to something. What was it? She also compared the rider's dress to something. What was it?

The make-believe fairy princesses you read about are usually beautiful. The stars you see from earth are bright, and they sparkle. That is what Rosalie meant when she compared the bareback rider to a princess and the dress to the stars. She meant the bareback rider was very beautiful, and she meant that the dress was bright and sparkling.

Quentin used a figure of speech to talk about the people on the flying trapeze.

"I loved the Flying Fosdicks!" said Quentin. "They were birds!"

The Flying Fosdicks can't fly the way real birds can. But they do swing through the air in their trapeze act. Quentin compared the Flying Fosdicks to something. What was it? His figure of speech compared the people to birds. He meant that the Fosdicks fly through the air like birds.

274

Practice

Here are some more things Rosalie said about the circus. Find the four figures of speech that Rosalie used. What two things are being compared in each figure of speech? What do you think each figure of speech means?

1. "The lion tamer put her head in a lion's mouth. The lion just sat there like a statue!"
2. "The strong man lifted the clown's car. He had arms as large as tree trunks."
3. "The horses were graceful. Each horse was a dancer with four legs."
4. "The clowns were very funny. They were as silly as monkeys."

As you read the next story, "My Grandpa and Me," you may find figures of speech. Think about the two things that are being compared. How are they alike?

My Grandpa and Me

by Patricia Lee Gauch

Grandpa and I like summertime best. We like
packing the car, squishing everything in. We
come to the cottage at night, and the windows
look yellow and warm. The cottage has a long,
long porch, and it sits on a bluff by the lake.

But it's what we do there that's special
for Grandpa and me.

276

In the morning we walk to the beach when there's no one there but us. The sun's just up and the sand's still cool between our toes. The lake's still calm.

There's a kind of quiet we like to hear—crying gulls and freighters' horns and waves along the beach. We listen and we walk.

There are tracks on the sand in the morning,
from gulls and pipers, from crabs and spiders.
There are tracks like three-pronged forks and
beads and wispy strings that seem to scurry—and
to stop. Sometimes we follow the tracks until
they disappear.

Sometimes we collect rocks. We name them pud-
ding stones and piano stones, pepper rocks and
flower stones. I can skip flat rocks two times,
three times. But Grandpa can skip them six,
seven, eight times when the lake's still asleep
and the waves are soft.

We build castles, too, when the sun's up. We use shells for turrets and bark for towers and sticks to spike the walls. Our castles have winding roads and moats and secret tunnels, in case our kings must escape in the night.

Sometimes our castles last TWO days, because no one likes to step on a castle as grand as ours.

When the sun gets hot we sit on the porch and drink lemonade. We play games like checkers and ticktacktoe. And I win sometimes. But if it's not too hot, we hike the trails Grandpa's made in the woods.

We look for meadowlarks and cardinals and goldfinches. (Grandpa knows the name of any bird; I know a robin and a cardinal for sure.)

And we look for certain trees like birch and hickory and white-pine trees. But I like to find the sugar maple best. It is an umbrella in the middle of the woods. That's where our secret berry patch is. We check our berries almost every day. When they're red and plump and juicy, we pick them. We save a bucket for the family, but mostly we sit right there and eat them.

Sometimes late in the afternoon, storms come up.

Grandpa says they're summer storms. They rumble from the west, in great angry puffs. We watch them from the porch as they come. The closer one gets, the quieter it gets. The wind stops blowing and the leaves hang still, waiting.

Then the storm breaks and it crashes around us. The rain pours down hard and loud on the roof. Sometimes it keeps blowing across the lake.

We see the lightning stab the water in bright flashes. We see the wind whip the waves and send them rolling across the beach, and we feel safe on our long porch.

At twilight the fish come in toward shore to feed. If the weather's good, we row to a quiet spot to catch them. But I'm not one for putting worms on hooks. And I don't think Grandpa's one for catching any poor fish. Mainly we sit out in the lake. We put our toes in the water and talk.

Skills Unit 15

When the sky grows dark, we let the boat
float ashore and watch the stars come out. They
seem so close.

We find the Dippers first, then the Bear and
the Dog. The Milky Way's easiest for me because
it looks like a pail of stars just spilled across
the sky.

Then, for a while, we watch the lake. It's
as black as the sky at night except for the
freighters. They light up from bow to stern and
look like strings of diamonds passing by.

For a while we watch, but bedtime comes.
It's always too early for me unless I get to
crawl in bed with Grandpa. The sheets are cold
and kind of clammy, and sometimes I can smell
the waves.

When the light goes out, and the room's pitch
dark, Grandpa says, "Let's trade stories." We do
and I forget about everything else.

Then, when we're done, we just listen to the
crickets and the waves. We listen to the
freighters' horns and we sleep.

Comprehension Check

1. What are some of the special things the boy does with his grandfather?
2. Where is the summer cottage located?
3. Why do you think the boy and his grandfather don't catch any fish?
4. Do you think the boy and his grandfather are good friends? Why do you think as you do?
5. Suppose you were the boy in the story. What other things would you like to do with the grandfather in the story?

Skill Check

Here are some things the boy in the story "My Grandpa and Me" said. Find the four figures of speech he used. What two things are being compared in each figure of speech below? What do you think each figure of speech means?

1. There are tracks like three-pronged forks.
2. The maple tree is an umbrella in the middle of the woods.
3. The Milky Way looks like a pail of stars spilled across the sky.
4. The freighters look like strings of diamonds passing by.

Literary Unit

The Skates of Uncle Richard

by Carol Fenner

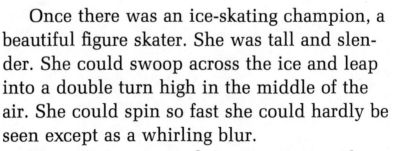

Once there was an ice-skating champion, a beautiful figure skater. She was tall and slender. She could swoop across the ice and leap into a double turn high in the middle of the air. She could spin so fast she could hardly be seen except as a whirling blur.

Her picture was in the newspaper on the sports page. Television cameras followed her around while she skated.

But there was only one person who knew where she lived. A girl named Marsha knew—because the beautiful figure skater lived inside Marsha's head.

Marsha was an eight-year-old girl who dreamed of many things. But most of all, she dreamed of being a figure skater. Marsha had watched the champion skaters on television since she was six. A part of her always skated with the skaters she watched.

Marsha herself had never skated with real ice skates on real ice. She would stand alone in her room, her arms lifted in the empty air. She would bend forward and extend one leg behind.

Marsha's ninth birthday was on its way, and she began to hint to her mother that she would like ice skates for her birthday.

On her birthday, Marsha got many presents. Her eyes flew over the piles of packages to a large box covered with red paper.

She couldn't bring herself to open the red box right away. First she opened a flat box and saw a new plaid dress. There were two new books for her. But her mind was on the box covered with red paper. Finally the present covered with red paper was the only one left to open.

She tore at the paper. The box inside looked like the one her last year's winter boots had come in. When she opened it up, there, inside the tissue, bulged the ugliest ice skates she had ever seen.

For a while Marsha just sat staring at the skates. Then slowly she took them out of the box. They were old-fashioned hockey skates, black with brown leather around the thick toes and brown circles at the ankles. Although the blades were clean and shining, the skates had obviously been used and used and used before.

"They were your Uncle Richard's," said her mother. "They were his skates when he was seven. He was about your size then. He took good care of them. They're almost good as new."

Marsha kept her eyes on the skates. She could
feel tears building up.

"Your uncle Richard is a fine skater," her
mother continued. "He learned how to skate on
those skates. They'll be a good start for you,
Marsha, till we see how you take to skating."

Marsha sat on the floor with the box at her
side, the ugly skates in her lap. "I remembered packing them away in the attic years
ago," her mother was saying. "Richard will be
pleased to know they're being used."

Marsha was feeling the beautiful skating
champion inside her head disappear. Her dream
of being a figure skater deserted her as the
ugliest skates in the world lay in her lap.

After Marsha's birthday, the skater never appeared whole and beautiful as before. Marsha stuffed Uncle Richard's skates way back in her closet, but it didn't help.

Then, one Saturday morning several weeks after her birthday, she went to her closet and took out the ugly skates. She sat on her bed and tried them on. They were actually a pretty good fit. She stood up on them. Her ankles wobbled. "It's because there's no ice," she thought. "It'll be all right if there's ice."

294

At lunchtime she asked her older brother,
Leonard, if he would take her to the lagoon.
He didn't really want to, but he said OK.

When they reached the lagoon, Marsha saw all
sizes of shoes and boots scattered near the
benches on the bank. They sat on a cold bench to
put on their skates. Leonard laced up rapidly,
whistling. He waved to some friends skating out
on the lagoon and said to Marsha impatiently,
"Hurry up, will you?"

She finally got her skates laced and stood
up. Her feet didn't feel as if they could fly
across the ice. They felt like blocks of wood.
She took a step and the skates suddenly slipped
away as if they were trying to escape from her
feet. Up into the air went her legs. Down into
the snow went Marsha.

"Oh, Marsha!" cried Leonard. He helped her up. Then he guided her down the bank to the ice. Nervously, Marsha stepped down onto the ice.

Whoooooooosh! Up into the air went Uncle Richard's skates. Down went Marsha onto the ice.

When Leonard helped her up again, Marsha pushed onto her ankles and stayed in one spot. It was no fun. Leonard kept looking around for his friends. Marsha kept falling down. Her ankles began to ache dreadfully. She was sore all over. Finally Leonard dragged her to a bench and left her there. "I'll be right back," he said and skated away to talk with his friends.

Marsha sat on the bench alone. She wanted to go home. She dropped her head. She felt cold and miserable.

The scraping sound of ice skates stopping suddenly made her look up. A man was standing in front of her, smiling. She was so wrapped up in unhappiness that at first she didn't know him. Then she recognized her uncle Richard.

He was saying, "Marsha girl, is that you? Why are you looking so sad?" Then he looked at her skates. "Why don't you lace up your skates properly?" he asked.

"They were your first skates when you were seven," Marsha said in a low voice.

Uncle Richard knelt down in front of her and said with delight, "They sure were . . . those good old skates!" Then he began to undo the laces, saying, "First off, Marsha, you've got to have your skates laced properly."

After he had finished lacing both skates, Uncle Richard stood her up and began to pull her slowly and evenly across the ice. "Bend your knees, not your middle," he told her. Marsha bent her knees and her middle straightened right up. She was surprised at how easily she could balance now.

After they had gone a short distance, Uncle Richard said, "You do that very well. Now I want to show you some things to practice while I get some skating done." First he showed Marsha how to rest her ankles when they got tired.

Then he said, "Here's something else to practice." He pushed forward onto one foot and trailed the other behind lightly without touching the ice. Then he brought the other foot forward and pushed easily onto that one. "I push," he said, "and then I glide . . . and then I push with the other foot. And then I glide!" Uncle Richard glided forward, first on one foot and then the other.

"Now you practice that for a while. Practice resting your ankles too whenever they get tired. OK?"

Marsha nodded and Uncle Richard skated off. She watched to see if he really could skate as well as her mother had said.

Slowly at first, Uncle Richard moved across the ice. Then Marsha saw him reach into his pocket and pull out a tiny radio. He held it next to his ear and began to skate to the music from the radio. First he made some smooth, neat turns. Then his speed quickened. He circled into a spin that blurred his entire outline.

Alone in the middle of the ice, Marsha felt her ankles begin to wobble. She tried resting them. It worked. They stopped wobbling. "But I can't stand here forever," she thought. She took a few timid steps. She skidded a little. She glided a little. She stopped and rested.

300

Then she took a deep breath, bent her knees, and pushed off onto her right foot the way Uncle Richard had done. She glided a little, her body balanced over her skating foot. Then she shifted and pushed onto her left foot. It worked! Push, glide . . . push, glide. She brought her legs together and glided on both feet all by herself.

She gasped with excitement. It was fun! She tried it again. She pushed off more boldly and glided farther. She did it over again and again.

Suddenly she realized she was at the other end of the lagoon. "My, my," said a voice behind her. "I thought I left you down at the other end." It was Uncle Richard. "How'd you get here?" he asked.

"I push-glided, push-glided," said Marsha. "All by myself."

"You are one surprising young lady," said Uncle Richard. "You sure learn fast." Marsha was surprised herself. He bent down and looked seriously into her face. "Are you ready for another suggestion?" he asked.

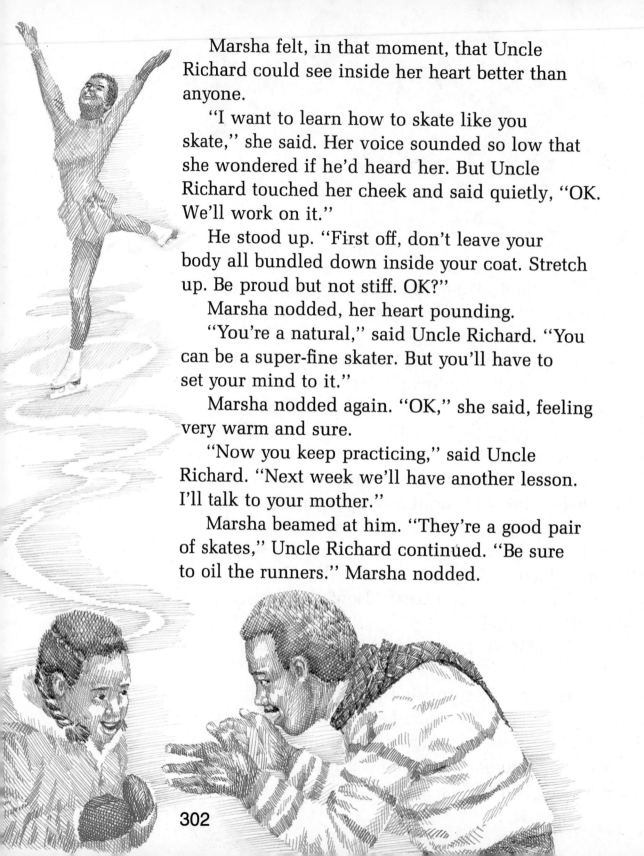

Marsha felt, in that moment, that Uncle Richard could see inside her heart better than anyone.

"I want to learn how to skate like you skate," she said. Her voice sounded so low that she wondered if he'd heard her. But Uncle Richard touched her cheek and said quietly, "OK. We'll work on it."

He stood up. "First off, don't leave your body all bundled down inside your coat. Stretch up. Be proud but not stiff. OK?"

Marsha nodded, her heart pounding.

"You're a natural," said Uncle Richard. "You can be a super-fine skater. But you'll have to set your mind to it."

Marsha nodded again. "OK," she said, feeling very warm and sure.

"Now you keep practicing," said Uncle Richard. "Next week we'll have another lesson. I'll talk to your mother."

Marsha beamed at him. "They're a good pair of skates," Uncle Richard continued. "Be sure to oil the runners." Marsha nodded.

Uncle Richard pushed off. Marsha watched him glide away. She pushed after him, her head high, her body stretched taller. Push, glide . . . push, glide. She skated past her staring brother. She hardly even wobbled. Proudly, not stiffly, Marsha glided away on the skates of Uncle Richard, taller and taller and taller.

Comprehension Check

1. What did Marsha dream about?
2. What did Marsha see when she opened the red box? How did she feel about it?
3. Why do you think Marsha stuffed the skates in her closet?
4. Who do you think was the better teacher, Leonard or Uncle Richard? Tell why you think as you do.
5. Do you think Marsha's dream will come true one day? Why do you think as you do?
6. Have you ever learned to skate or do another sport? How long did it take? Who helped you?

THINKING

by Felice Holman

Silently
Inside my head
Behind my eyes
A thought begins to grow and be
A part of me.
And then I think
I always knew
The thing I only got to know,
As though it always
Was right there
Inside my head
Behind my eyes
Where I keep things.

Patsy and the C.B.

by Monica Gallagher

Patsy Wesaw stared out of the car window. She hardly noticed the fog. She was thinking about going to the Cherokee reservation where her grandmother lived. It was Grandma's ninetieth birthday, and Patsy's family was having a big party for her. It would be great seeing everyone again—aunts, uncles, and cousins. But if Patsy's father treated her like a baby, it would spoil everything.

"Dad? You won't treat me like a baby, will you?" asked Patsy.

"What, Kitten?" said Mr. Wesaw. He didn't take his eyes off the road. The fog was getting worse every minute.

"Oh, Dad! If you call me baby names in front of everyone, I'll just die! My name is *Patsy*, not Kitten," she said.

306

"Sure, Kitten," Mr. Wesaw said. Then he lifted the speaker of the Citizens Band radio and spoke into it. "10–13. This is Sky Hawk. I'm going east on Judd Highway coming up to the Ogden exit. How's the weather around there?"

The answer came back, "This is Little Fox. You're running into heavy fog. Take it slow, good buddy, and be careful."

Mr. Wesaw slowed the car down. "I'm going to stop on the side of the road and give the fog a chance to pass," he said.

Patsy's father brought the car to a stop. Patsy unfastened her seat belt and started to open the car door. Suddenly the car was hit hard from behind! Patsy was thrown out of the car as it was pushed off the roadside and down a steep hill. With a crash, the car came to a rest against a large rock.

For a long moment Patsy lay still. Then she sat up and reached for her father. But she discovered that she had been thrown from the car, and she couldn't see it because of the fog.

Patsy started screaming. "Dad! Dad!" But there was no answer. Afraid, Patsy stood up in the fog trying to see her father.

Then she heard it—the sound of the C.B. radio. Patsy remembered that the radio had been on when the car was hit. She began to walk toward the sound, listening as it grew louder and louder.

Soon the big shadow of the car appeared in the fog. With her heart pounding, Patsy pulled open the door. Her father was slumped in his seat. His eyes were closed and he looked pale. But he was breathing.

Patsy knew she had to get help. She would have to use the C.B.

Patsy had seen her father use it many times. She didn't understand the special language he used when he was speaking to someone on the C.B. But she was sure she could use it to get help anyway.

In a shaking voice, she called into the speaker, "This is Patsy Wesaw. My father has been hurt in an accident. Please, somebody, help us."

At once a voice said, "Your 10–33 received, Patsy. What's your 10–20?" Patsy didn't understand. Then the voice explained, "Where are you?"

Patsy remembered what her father had told Little Fox just before the car was hit. She gave the information and was told, "If you've got any flares in the car, light them. I'll give your message to Smokey—that's the police. Help will be there in no time."

Just then Mr. Wesaw began to open his eyes. He sat up slowly. "I'm all right, Kitten," he said. "Just a little shaken."

Patsy explained what had happened. Then she told him to lie still while she got the flares from the trunk of the car. She lighted them as she had seen her father do before.

Soon the police arrived. Patsy and her father were taken to the hospital to make sure they weren't hurt. Luckily both of them were fine, so they decided to go on to Grandma's party.

When they arrived, Grandma looked at Patsy and said, "My, what a big girl our Kitten is!"

"Yes," said Mr. Wesaw, smiling proudly, "but her name is Patsy."

Comprehension Check

1. Where were Patsy and her father going? Why were they going there?
2. Why did Mr. Wesaw make a call on the C.B.?
3. What happened when Mr. Wesaw brought the car to a stop? Why do you think the other driver didn't stop?
4. Do you think Patsy is a brave girl? Tell why you think as you do.
5. What safety rules do you know that can help prevent accidents?

Skill Check

Think about what the characters said and did in the story to answer the following questions.

1. How did Patsy feel about being called "Kitten"? How can you tell?
2. How did Patsy feel when she spoke into the C.B. radio? How do you know?
3. Was Mr. Wesaw proud of Patsy after the accident? How can you tell?

Listening in on C.B.

by Linda Everstz

Many people have discovered a new way of
communicating. They can do it anywhere—in a
car, at home, even in a restaurant. What is
this great discovery? The C.B., or Citizens
Band radio.

C.B. radios first became popular with truck
drivers in 1974. Today many people who drive
cars use C.B. radios. For people on the move,
a C.B. radio set can be a useful tool.

People use C.B. radios for many reasons. Most
people use their radios to make driving safer.
They swap information about the weather, the
condition of the road, and traffic. They use
C.B. radios to call for help in case of an emergency. Truck drivers who drive long distances
find that having a C.B. helps keep them awake
and prevents them from becoming bored.

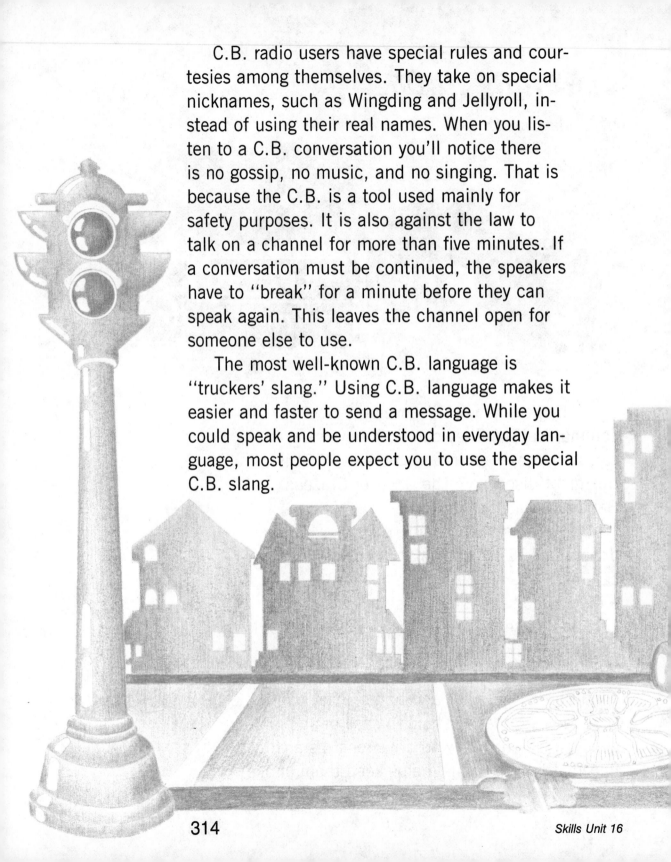

C.B. radio users have special rules and courtesies among themselves. They take on special nicknames, such as Wingding and Jellyroll, instead of using their real names. When you listen to a C.B. conversation you'll notice there is no gossip, no music, and no singing. That is because the C.B. is a tool used mainly for safety purposes. It is also against the law to talk on a channel for more than five minutes. If a conversation must be continued, the speakers have to "break" for a minute before they can speak again. This leaves the channel open for someone else to use.

The most well-known C.B. language is "truckers' slang." Using C.B. language makes it easier and faster to send a message. While you could speak and be understood in everyday language, most people expect you to use the special C.B. slang.

Here are some examples of C.B. slang. Read the lists carefully. Then see if you can figure out the C.B. conversation on the next page.

When C.B. Users Say:	They Mean:
break 1–9	request to talk on Channel 19
adios	a sign off, good-by
come back	please answer
10–4	I hear and understand
baloneys	tires
nap trap	rest area
skating rink	slippery road
collect call	call for a certain person using the C.B.

"Break 1–9. This is Wingding. I have a collect call for Jellyroll. Come back."

"This is Jellyroll. I'm listening."

"10–4. One of my baloneys is flat. Meet me at the nap trap on Route Three. Come back."

"10–4, Wingding. I'm on a skating rink now and have to move slowly. Will see you at the nap trap on Route Three as soon as possible. Adios."

In everyday English this would read:

"I want to talk on Channel Nineteen. This is Wingding. I want to talk to Jellyroll. Please answer."

"This is Jellyroll. I'm listening."

"I hear you. One of my tires is flat. Meet me at the rest area on Route Three. Please answer."

"I understand you, Wingding. The road is slippery here and I have to move slowly. I'll see you at the rest area on Route Three as soon as possible. Good-by."

Comprehension Check

1. What kinds of information do C.B. users exchange on their radios?
2. Why is there no gossip, music, or singing on C.B. radios?
3. Do you think the C.B. radio is a good tool? Why do you think as you do?
4. What other uses can you think of for C.B. radios?

Identifying the Order of Events

Sometimes it is important to know the order in which events happen in a story. The order is also important when you are following directions. Read the next story. Pay attention to the order of events and to the steps in the directions Andrea followed.

Andrea found a seed in her grapefruit juice.

"Why don't you plant it?" said her father. "There's a book in the living room that will tell you how to do it."

Andrea got the book and started reading. Here is what she read:

1. Fill a pot with soil.
2. Plant the seed one inch (about 2½ centimeters) deep. in a pot filled w/soil
3. Water the soil but do not soak it.
4. Put the pot in the sunlight.
5. Water the soil when it gets dry.

Andrea followed the directions. Soon something small and green poked up through the dirt. Then a stem and two tiny leaves appeared. Finally Andrea showed the pot to her father. "Look!" she cried. "I've got a plant!"

What was the first thing that happened in the story? Andrea found a grapefruit seed in her juice. What happened next? Andrea planted the seed. What was the last thing that happened?

Andrea's seed grew because she followed the directions in the plant book. The order of the directions was very important.

Suppose Andrea had not followed the directions. What might have happened?

Practice

Read the paragraph below and answer the questions that follow.

It was Lee's birthday. She wanted to do something special. She wanted to make spaghetti—her favorite food. She asked her grandfather to help her.

What do you think Lee and her grandfather did first, second, third, and last?
a. Pour the cooked spaghetti into a strainer.
b. Boil the spaghetti for seven minutes.
c. Boil a potful of water.
d. Add the spaghetti to the boiling water.

As you read the next stories, "Merlin and Merlin" and "The Magic Tube," pay attention to the order of events. The order will help you understand each story.

MERLIN AND MERLIN

by Linda Berry

Jeff's eyes were on the lamp across the
room. He said, "And now, ladies and gentlemen,
when the dragon speaks Merlin's magic words,
he will escape from his prison. Snik! Snak!
Snorum!"

The cardboard dragon slid out of its cardboard cage. Jeff bowed to the lamp and sighed
happily. He had finally done that trick right!

Four houses away, Christine stood behind a table. She spoke loudly, carefully watching herself in the mirror. "You saw me remove the coin from the box," she said. "Now I will close the box and say Merlin's magic word. And the coin will be back in the box. Abracadabra!"

She opened the box again to show a shiny coin. Good! That would be the last trick in her act.

The next day Jeff and Christine were surprised to see each other at the tryouts for the school talent show. They carried the same kinds of boxes called "Merlin's Magic Kit."

When Christine's turn came, Jeff watched jealously. She was doing *his* tricks! He saw that the quick-moving tricks seemed to go more smoothly for Christine than they did for him.

Christine tried to study Jeff's magic act while appearing to look out the window. She saw that his black cape and smooth talk covered the hard part of more than one trick.

After they finished, Mr. Mayahara called Christine and Jeff. He said, "You both did a very good job. But we can have only one magic act in the show. We'll decide and let you know tomorrow."

Jeff muttered to himself all the way home. "I wish there were *real* magic in this box, instead of cardboard. I'd fix her. Using *my* tricks!" But he really was a little worried.

Christine was worried too. "I wonder if a cape would help? I know I do the string-and-ring tricks better than he does. But I wish I were better at the smooth talk."

By the next morning Jeff thought he had found an answer to the problem.

"Christine!" he called, when he saw her on the playground. "I've figured out a way we can both be in the show. I'll be the magician, and you can be my assistant. Magicians always have assistants."

He could tell right away that Christine wasn't pleased. "Not on your magic wand, Merlin Smerlin!" she said. "I'm as good a magician as you are. I don't plan to let *you* do *my* act!"

They stood glaring at each other. Then a thoughtful gleam came into Christine's eyes. "Wait a minute," she said slowly. "You may almost have a good idea there. We might make a good *team*.

"You'll have to agree that I'm better at doing the quick-moving tricks," Christine said. It was true, but Jeff didn't want to say so. He kept quiet and let her talk.

Christine went on. "And you are better with the chatter."

Jeff nodded, still listening. That was definitely true.

"We could work out an act so we could both do what we do best," Christine said. "Equal partners."

"That's not a bad idea," Jeff said. He wished he had thought of it himself. "Yeah. Partners. We could be 'Jeff and Christine—the Magic Duo.'"

A cold look came into Christine's eyes. "You mean 'Christine and Jeff—the Magic Duo,'" she said.

"How about 'Merlin and Merlin'?" Jeff asked. "That way nobody could tell whose name comes first."

Christine smiled at him. "Let's go talk to
Mr. Mayahara," she said. "If it's OK with him,
we'll get to work on our act."

Mr. Mayahara seemed happy that Christine and
Jeff had decided to work together. "Wonderful!"
he said.

And wonderful it was! Merlin and Merlin was the hit of the talent show. It was unusual to see two magicians working together. Jeff's smooth talk and Christine's quick-moving tricks made a fine show.

"Two heads are better than one," said Merlin.

And the other Merlin added, "And in this case, two acts were better than one!"

Comprehension Check

1. What kinds of tricks were Jeff and Christine practicing? Why?
2. Why do you think Christine didn't like the idea of being Jeff's assistant?
3. Do you think Jeff was being fair when he expected Christine to be his assistant? Why or why not?
4. Do you think the magic act was better because Jeff and Christine did it together? Explain why you think as you do.
5. Have you ever done anything in cooperation with others? Was it easier to do the job?

Skill Check

Which of the following events from the story happened first, second, third, and last?
a. Jeff asked Christine to be his assistant.
b. They saw each other at the tryouts.
c. They became equal partners in the show.
d. They practiced their acts separately.

The Magic Tube

by Barbara Seuling

In the story "Merlin and Merlin," Christine
made a coin disappear and reappear. You can do
a trick like Christine's. In this trick you put
a secret lid over the rim of a glass to hide the
coin. When you lift the glass, the coin seems
to reappear.

To do the trick, you will need:
    a glass
    a coin larger than a dime
    1 large piece of colored paper
    2 large pieces of white paper
    glue
    scissors
    a pencil

328

Glass with Secret Lid Put the glass upside down on one sheet of white paper. Draw a circle on the paper around the top of the glass. Cut out the circle. Glue the circle to the rim of the glass.

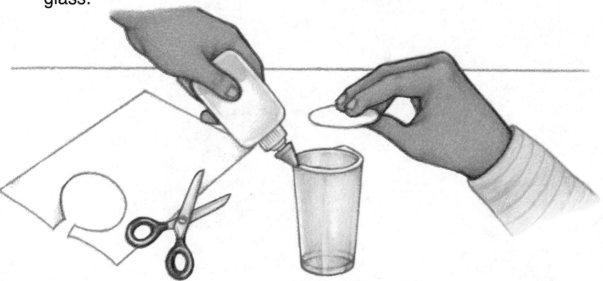

Magic Tube Roll the colored paper into a tube. The tube should be large enough to fit over the glass. Glue the tube so the paper won't unroll.

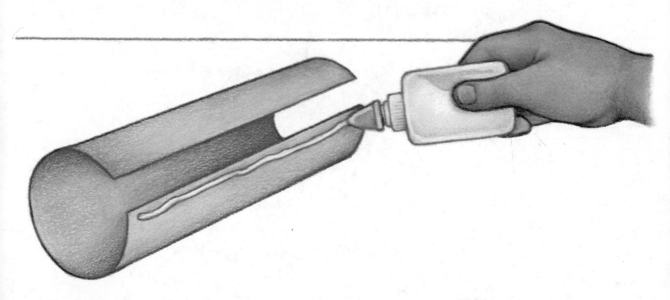

1. Put the glass and the tube on the other sheet of white paper. Put the glass upside down, as it is shown in the picture. Hold up the coin so everyone can see it. Then place it on the paper in front of the glass.

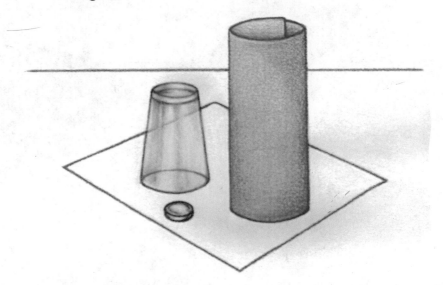

2. Lift the tube and place it over the glass. Hold the tube tightly against the glass. Lift the tube and the glass together and place them over the coin.

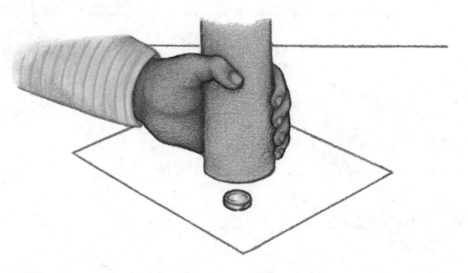

3. Lift off the tube. Do not lift the glass. The coin is gone! The secret is that the coin is under the fake lid on the glass. The fake lid hides the coin.

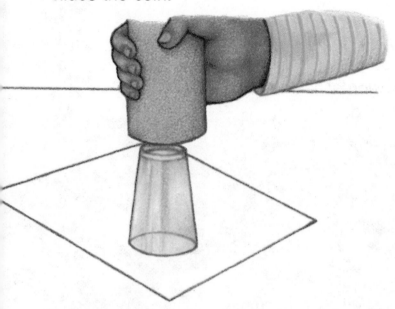

4. Place the tube back over the glass. Again, lift the glass with the tube. The coin reappears!

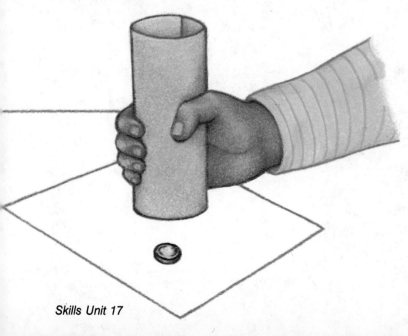

Be sure you do not lift the glass without using the tube. The fake lid would show. When the glass is resting on the white paper, the lid will not show.

Make up some smooth chatter like Jeff's to say as you do the trick. Don't forget to say some magic words! Then try the trick on your family and friends.

Comprehension Check

1. What are the things you need for Christine's trick?
2. Why is it important to lift the glass using the tube?
3. What would you do to prepare yourself before you try the trick on your family or friends? Explain why.
4. What magic words can you think of to say as you do the trick?

Skill Check

What did Christine do first, second, third, and last in her magic act?

a. She lifted the glass with the tube and placed it over the coin.
b. She lifted off only the tube, making the coin disappear.
c. She put the tube back over the glass and lifted the glass with the tube. The coin reappeared!
d. She placed the coin on the paper in front of the glass.

The Answer-Backer Cure

by Betty MacDonald

At three o'clock in the afternoon, Mrs. O'Toole put a peanut-butter sandwich and a glass of cold milk on the kitchen table for her son when he came home from school. Pretty soon the front door slammed and in bounced Gary. His mother asked, "How was school, dear?"

After drinking his milk, Gary said, "Well, this afternoon Mrs. Morse said, 'Gary O'Toole will stay in at recess and put the paint boxes away,' and I said, 'You're the teacher here, Mrs. Morse. Why don't you put the paint boxes away and let me go out and play?' Everybody in the whole room laughed, but Mrs. Morse didn't think it was so funny."

Mrs. O'Toole was shocked. She said, "That was a very rude thing for you to do, Gary. I am ashamed of you. When you finish your sandwich and milk, you had better go up to your room and stay there until dinner."

Gary pulled his mouth down at the corners, squinted up his eyes, and said, "Why should I?" He kept his mouth pulled down and blinked his eyes rapidly in a most disagreeable way.

Mrs. O'Toole was dumbfounded. Never had Gary acted this way before. She said quietly, "You should because I tell you to."

Gary walked slowly out of the kitchen. When he reached the top of the stairs, he called down to his mother, "I'm going because I want to, but not because you tell me to," and dashed into his room.

The next morning his mother said, "Please hurry with your breakfast, Gary. You'll be late for school."

Gary pulled his mouth down and began blinking. He said, "I'm the one that's eating this breakfast!" Gary's mother shook her head and was about to say something as Gary grabbed his sweater and slammed out the front door.

Mrs. O'Toole thought that she had better call Mrs. Piggle-Wiggle. Mrs. Piggle-Wiggle lived down the street and knew more about children than anybody in the neighborhood. Mrs. O'Toole rushed to the telephone and called Mrs. Piggle-Wiggle. She said, "Oh, Mrs. Piggle-Wiggle, I am so worried about my son, Gary."

Mrs. Piggle-Wiggle said, "I know Gary. He has such nice brown eyes."

Mrs. O'Toole said, "Well, his eyes don't look nice anymore. He squints them up, pulls down his mouth, and then blinks."

Mrs. Piggle-Wiggle said, "He answers back and is rude, isn't he?"

Mrs. O'Toole said, "Yes, he is. But how did you know?"

Mrs. Piggle-Wiggle said, "I can recognize the answer-backer symptoms. Some of the most charming children I know were once answer-backers. You drop by here after lunch and I will give you Penelope. Penelope is a cure for even the most stubborn cases of answer-backishness."

Right after lunch Mrs. O'Toole went down to Mrs. Piggle-Wiggle's house and got Penelope. Penelope Parrot was a large, cross-looking green bird who blinked rapidly. Mrs. Piggle-Wiggle said, as she handed the cage to Mrs. O'Toole, "Fortunately for you, Penelope will only talk to children."

During the walk home from Mrs. Piggle-Wiggle's house, Penelope was quiet and looked very cross. When Mrs. O'Toole hung her cage in the kitchen, she hunched down and put her head under her wing. But when Gary came in from school, Penelope woke up. Gary was delighted with Penelope. He said, "Oh, Mother, I've always wanted a parrot. Do you think she can talk?"

Mrs. O'Toole said, "I was told that she speaks only to children."

Gary said, "Where did you get her, Mother?"

His mother said, "I'm keeping her for a friend of mine. When you play in your room, you may hang her cage by the window, if you'd like."

338

Gary brought his milk and cookies over by Penelope's cage and was very surprised when Penelope blinked and said rudely, "Give me a bite." Gary broke off a piece of the cookie. Penelope snatched it and ate it without a word of thanks.

Gary turned to his mother. "She's certainly not very polite, is she?"

His mother said, "Perhaps she has only been around rude people. After all, she is only a parrot and repeats what she hears."

Gary was excited about Penelope and wanted to show her to some of the neighborhood children. "May I bring my friends in to see her, Mother?" he asked.

Before Mrs. O'Toole could answer, Penelope began hopping up and down, blinking and yelling.

Gary's mother said, "If you are not more polite, Penelope, I'll put a cloth over your cage."

Gary asked excitedly, "What will that do to Penelope?"

Mrs. O'Toole said, "If I put a cloth over her cage, she will think that it is night and go to sleep."

Penelope squawked, "I'll do it because I want to, but not because you tell me to!"

Gary was certainly surprised at that, because he thought that he had made up that brilliant remark. He didn't dare look at his mother, so he went out to find his friends.

340

Before dinner Mrs. O'Toole said to Gary, "Gary, dear, send your friends home now. It is time for you to do your homework." Gary turned to his mother and began pulling down his mouth, squinting his eyes, and blinking.

But before he could say a word, Penelope yelled at Gary, "Say, who's the boss around here?"

Gary's mother quickly put a cloth over her cage and politely asked the children to leave.

After dinner Mrs. O'Toole hung Penelope's cage in Gary's room. Penelope squawked and made so much noise that Gary finally said, "Oh, be quiet!"

And Penelope blinked and said, "I'll do it because I want to, but not because you tell me to." Gary got into bed quickly and turned off the light.

The next morning Gary was very slow. He could not find one of his socks and he couldn't button his shirt. Finally his mother called, "Gary, hurry, dear, breakfast is waiting!"

Gary pulled down his mouth and squinted up his eyes and said, "Oh, hurry yourself!"

Penelope jerked up her head and said, "Oh, hurry yourself, slowpoke. Hurry!"

Gary said crossly, "Oh, be quiet, Penelope!"

Penelope said, "I'll do it because I want to, but not because you tell me to. Say, who's the boss around here? Oh yeah?"

Gary ran downstairs and sat down to breakfast. Mrs. O'Toole ran upstairs and got Penelope and hung her cage by the kitchen window.

When the children called for Gary and Mrs. O'Toole said, "Hurry, dear, you will make your friends late for school," Gary pulled down his mouth and squinted up his eyes and blinked.

But before he could say a word, Penelope squawked at Gary, "I'm the one who's eating this breakfast! Hurry yourself, slowpoke!"

Gary was ashamed to look at his mother, so he rushed off. Penelope yelled after him, "Hurry, slowpoke. Bell's ringing!"

When Gary came home from school that afternoon he kissed his mother and said, "Mother, I apologized to Mrs. Morse today, and she said that next week I may be monitor for the scissors."

Penelope yelled, "Who said so? Who's the
boss?"

Gary turned to Penelope and said, "You are
a very rude bird. If you don't hush right now
I will put the cloth over your cage."

Penelope blinked and said, "Hush! That's all
I hear. I'll do it because I want to, but not
because you tell me to."

Gary's mother said, "I think it is time you
went home, Penelope. Gary, would you like to
return Penelope to Mrs. Piggle-Wiggle?"

Gary said, "Oh, yes, Mother. And may I stay
and play?"

Mrs. O'Toole said, "I think you had better
come home and practice. Your music lesson is
tomorrow, you know."

Gary started to draw down his mouth, squint up his eyes, and blink, but suddenly he looked at Penelope. Then he turned up his mouth, opened his eyes, and smiled. He said, "All right, Mother. I'll come right home *after* I return that rude Penelope."

Comprehension Check

1. What did Gary do to make his mother call Mrs. Piggle-Wiggle?
2. Why do you think Mrs. Piggle-Wiggle lent Mrs. O'Toole the parrot?
3. How did the parrot cure Gary of his answer-backishness?
4. Do you think Mrs. Piggle-Wiggle's way of dealing with Gary's problem was right? Tell why or why not.
5. Suppose you were Gary's mother or father. How would you help him get over his answer-backishness?

Skill Check

Answer the two questions. Then tell what words complete the sentence.

1. In the story who is rude to children?
2. In the story who is rude to grownups?
3. Penelope is rude to _____ as Gary is rude to _____ .

AMOS and BORIS

by William Steig

Amos, a mouse, lived by the ocean. He loved
the ocean. He loved the smell of sea air. He
loved to hear the surf sounds—the bursting
breakers, the backwashes with rolling pebbles.

He thought a lot about the ocean, and he wondered about the faraway places on the other side of the water. One day he started building a boat on the beach. He worked on it in the daytime, while at night he studied navigation.

When the boat was finished, he loaded it with cheese, biscuits, acorns, honey, wheat germ, two barrels of fresh water, a compass, a sextant, a telescope, a saw, a hammer and nails and some wood in case repairs should be necessary, a needle and thread for the mending of torn sails, and various other necessities such as bandages and iodine, a yo-yo and dominoes.

On the sixth of September, with a very calm
sea, he waited till the high tide had almost
reached his boat; then, using his most savage
strength, he just managed to push the boat into
the water, climb on board, and set sail.

The *Rodent*, for that was the boat's name,
proved to be very well made and very well suited
to the sea. And Amos, after one miserable day
of seasickness, proved to be a natural sailor,
very well suited to the ship.

He was enjoying his trip immensely. It was
beautiful weather. Day and night he moved up and
down, up and down, on waves as big as mountains,
and he was full of wonder, full of enterprise, and
full of love for life.

One night, in a phosphorescent sea, he marveled at the sight of some whales spouting luminous water; and later, lying on the deck of his boat gazing at the immense, starry sky, the tiny mouse Amos, a little speck of a living thing in the vast living universe, felt thoroughly akin to it all. Overwhelmed by the beauty and mystery of everything, he rolled over and over and right off the deck of his boat and into the sea.

"Help!" he squeaked as he grabbed desperately at the *Rodent*. But it evaded his grasp and went bowling along under full sail, and he never saw it again.

And there he was! Where? In the middle of the immense ocean, a thousand miles from the nearest shore, with no one else in sight as far as the eye could see and not even so much as a stick of driftwood to hold on to. "Should I try to swim home?" Amos wondered. "Or should I just try to stay afloat?" He might swim a mile, but never a thousand. He decided to just keep afloat, treading water and hoping that something—who knows what?—would turn up to save him. But what if a shark, or some big fish, a horse mackerel, turned up? What was he supposed to do to protect himself? He didn't know.

Morning came, as it always does. He was getting terribly tired. He was a very small, very cold, very wet and worried mouse. There was still nothing in sight but the empty sea. Then, as if things weren't bad enough, it began to rain.

At last the rain stopped and the noonday sun gave him a bit of cheer and warmth in the vast loneliness; but his strength was giving out. He began to wonder what it would be like to drown. Would it take very long? Would it feel just awful?

As he was asking himself these dreadful questions, a huge head burst through the surface of the water and loomed up over him. It was a whale. "What sort of fish are you?" the whale asked. "You must be one of a kind!"

"I'm not a fish," said Amos. "I'm a mouse, which is a mammal. I live on land."

"Curly clams and cuttlefish!" said the whale. "I'm a mammal myself, though I live in the sea. Call me Boris," he added.

Amos introduced himself and told Boris how
he came to be there in the middle of the ocean.
The whale said he would be happy to take Amos to
the Ivory Coast of Africa, where he happened
to be headed anyway, to attend a meeting
of whales from all the seven seas. But Amos said
he'd had enough adventure to last him a while.
He wanted only to get back home and hoped the
whale wouldn't mind going out of his way to take
him there.

"Not only would I not mind," said Boris, "I would consider it a privilege. What other whale in all the world ever had the chance to get to know such a strange creature as you! Please climb aboard." And Amos got on Boris's back.

"Are you sure you're a mammal?" Amos asked. "You smell more like a fish." Then Boris the whale went swimming along, with Amos the mouse on his back.

What a relief to be so safe, so secure again! Amos lay down in the sun, and being worn to a frazzle, he was soon asleep.

Then all of a sudden he was in the water again, wide awake, spluttering and splashing about! Boris had forgotten for a moment that he had a passenger on his back and had sounded. When he realized his mistake, he surfaced so quickly that Amos was sent somersaulting, tail over whiskers, high into the air.

Hitting the water hurt. Crazy with rage, Amos screamed and punched at Boris until he remembered he owed his life to the whale and quietly climbed on his back. From then on, whenever Boris wanted to sound, he warned Amos in advance and got his okay, and whenever he sounded, Amos took a swim.

356

Swimming along, sometimes at great speed, sometimes slowly and leisurely, sometimes resting and exchanging ideas, sometimes stopping to sleep, it took them a week to reach Amos's home shore. During that time, they developed a deep admiration for one another. Boris admired the delicacy, the quivering daintiness, the light touch, the small voice, the gemlike radiance of the mouse. Amos admired the bulk, the grandeur, the power, the purpose, the rich voice, and the abounding friendliness of the whale.

They became the closest possible friends. They told each other about their lives, their ambitions. They shared their deepest secrets with each other. The whale was very curious about life on land and was sorry that he could never experience it. Amos was fascinated by the whale's accounts of what went on deep under the sea. Amos sometimes enjoyed running up and down on the whale's back for exercise. When he was hungry, he ate plankton. The only thing he missed was fresh, unsalty water.

The time came to say goodbye. They were at the shore. "I wish we could be friends forever," said Boris. "We *will* be friends forever, but we can't be together. You must live on land and I must live at sea. I'll never forget you, though."

"And you can be sure I'll never forget *you*," said Amos. "I will always be grateful to you for saving my life and I want you to remember that if you ever need my help I'd be more than glad to give it!" How he could ever possibly help Boris, Amos didn't know, but he knew how willing he was.

The whale couldn't take Amos all the way in to land. They said their last goodbye. and Amos dived off Boris's back and swam to the sand.

From the top of a cliff he watched Boris spout twice and disappear.

358

Boris laughed to himself. "How could that little mouse ever help me? Little as he is, he's all heart. I love him, and I'll miss him terribly."

Boris went to the conference off the Ivory Coast of Africa and then went back to a life of whaling about, while Amos returned to his life of mousing around. And they were both happy.

Many years after the incidents just described, when Amos was no longer a very young mouse, and when Boris was no longer a very young whale, there occurred one of the worst storms of the century, Hurricane Yetta; and it just so happened that Boris the whale was flung ashore by a tidal wave and stranded on the very shore where Amos happened to make his home.

It also just so happened that when the storm had cleared up and Boris was lying high and dry on the sand, losing his moisture in the hot sun and needing desperately to be back in the water, Amos came down to the beach to see how much damage Hurricane Yetta had done. Of course Boris and Amos recognized each other at once. I don't have to tell you how these old friends felt at meeting again in this desperate situation. Amos rushed toward Boris. Boris could only look at Amos.

"Amos, help me," said the mountain of a whale to the mote of a mouse. "I think I'll die if I don't get back in the water soon." Amos gazed at Boris in an agony of pity. He realized he had to do something very fast and had to think very fast about what it was he had to do. Suddenly he was gone.

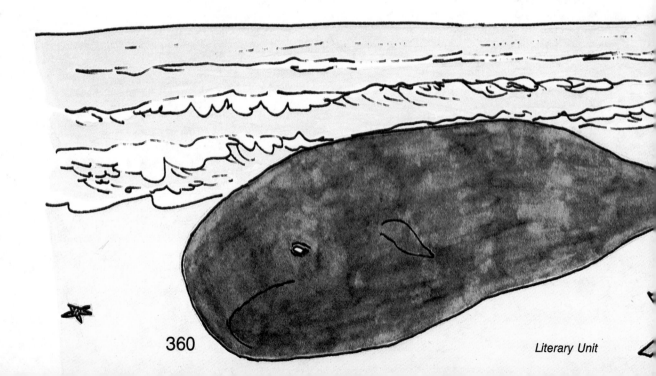

"I'm afraid he won't be able to help me,"
said Boris to himself. "Much as he wants to do
something, what can such a little fellow do?"

Just as Amos had once felt, all alone in the
middle of the ocean, Boris felt now, lying alone
on the shore. He was sure he would die. And just
as he was preparing to die, Amos came racing
back with two of the biggest elephants he could
find.

Without wasting time, these two goodhearted
elephants got to pushing with all their might at
Boris's huge body until he began turning over,
breaded with sand, and rolling down toward
the sea. Amos, standing on the head of one of
the elephants, yelled instructions, but no one
heard him.

In a few minutes Boris was already in water,
with waves washing at him, and he was feeling
the wonderful wetness. "You have to be out of
the sea really to know how good it is to be in it,"
he thought. "That is, if you're a whale." Soon
he was able to wiggle and wriggle into deeper
water.

He looked back at Amos on the elephant's head. Tears were rolling down the great whale's cheeks. The tiny mouse had tears in his eyes too. "Goodbye, dear friend," squeaked Amos. "Goodbye, dear friend," rumbled Boris, and he disappeared in the waves. They knew they might never meet again. They knew they would never forget each other.

Glossary

Full Pronunciation Key

The pronunciation of each word is shown just after the word, in this way:
ab bre vi ate (ə brē′vē āt).

The letters and signs used are pronounced as the words below.

The mark ′ is placed after a syllable with primary or heavy accent, as in the example above.

The mark ′ after a syllable shows a secondary or lighter accent, as in
ab bre vi ation (ə brē′vē a′shən).

a	hat, cap	**j**	jam, enjoy	**u**	cup, butter
ā	age, face	**k**	kind, seek	**u̇**	full, put
ä	father, far	**l**	land, coal	**ü**	rule, move
		m	me, am		
b	bad, rob	**n**	no, in	**v**	very, save
ch	child, much	**ng**	long, bring	**w**	will, woman
d	did, red			**y**	young, yet
		o	hot, rock	**z**	zero, breeze
e	let, best	**ō**	open, go	**zh**	measure, seizure
ē	equal, be	**ô**	order, all		
ėr	term, learn	**oi**	oil, voice		
		ou	house, out	**ə**	represents:
f	fat, if				a in about
g	go, bag	**p**	paper, cup		e in taken
h	he, how	**r**	run, try		i in pencil
		s	say, yes		o in lemon
i	it, pin	**sh**	she, rush		u in circus
ī	ice, five	**t**	tell, it		
		th	thin, both		
		ŦH	then, smooth		

A a

a hat	**i** it	**oi** oil	**ch** child		a in about
ā age	**ī** ice	**ou** out	**ng** long		e in taken
ä far	**o** hot	**u** cup	**sh** she	ə =	i in pencil
e let	**ō** open	**u̇** put	**th** thin		o in lemon
ē equal	**ô** order	**ü** rule	**ᴛʜ** then		u in circus
ėr term			**zh** measure		

ac ci den tal (ak′sə den′tl), happening by chance: *Breaking the lamp was accidental; I did not do it on purpose.* *adjective.*

ad mi ra tion (ad′mə rā′shən), the feeling we have when we think something or someone is very special: *I felt admiration for the woman who wrote such beautiful music.* *noun.*

aisle (īl), **1** any long, narrow passage. **2** passage between rows of seats in a hall, theater, or school. *noun.*

a larm (ə lärm′), **1** make afraid; frighten: *The breaking of a branch under my foot alarmed the deer.* **2** sudden fear; excitement caused by fear of danger: *The deer darted off in alarm.* **3** a warning of approaching danger: *The alarm went out that a tornado was approaching.* **4** a bell or other device that makes a noise to warn or waken people. **1** *verb,* **2,3,4** *noun.*

al ien (ā′lyən), **1** from another country or place: *French is an alien language to Americans.* **2** people who are not citizens of the country in which they live. **1** *adjective,* **2** *noun.*

an cient (ān′shənt), belonging to times long past: *In Egypt we saw the ruins of an ancient temple built six thousand years ago.* *adjective.*

an guish (ang′gwish), very great pain or grief: *He was in anguish until the doctor treated him.* *noun.*

anx ious (angk′shəs), **1** wishing very much; eager: *They were anxious to start their vacation.* **2** worried because of thoughts or fears of what may happen; troubled: *I felt anxious about my final exams.* *adjective.*

as pen (as′pən), a kind of poplar tree whose leaves tremble and rustle in the slightest breeze. *noun.*

a stride (ə strīd′), with one leg on either side of something: *He sat astride the horse.* *preposition.*

as tron o my (ə stron′ə mē), science that deals with the sun, moon, planets, stars, and other heavenly bodies. *noun.*

at tend ant (ə ten′dənt), **1** person who waits on another, such as a servant or follower. **2** waiting on another to help or serve: *An attendant nurse is at the patient's bedside.* **1** *noun,* **2** *adjective.*

av o ca do (av′ə kä′ dō), the fruit of a tree that grows in warm climates. Avocados are shaped like pears and have a dark-green skin and a very large seed. People often put avocados into salads. See picture. *noun, plural* **av o ca dos.**

avocado

B b

bas set (bas′it), a hunting dog with short legs and a long, heavy body. *noun.*

Bir ming ham (bėr′ming ham), a city in the central part of the state of Alabama.

bound ar y (boun′dər ē), limit; border; the line that divides one country, place, or thing from another country, place, or thing: *Lake Superior forms part of the boundary between Canada and the United States.* *noun, plural* **bound ar ies.**

bow[1] (bou), the front part of a ship or boat. *noun.*

bow[2] (bou), **1** bend the head or body in greeting, respect, or worship: *The people bowed before the queen.* **2** a bending of the head or body: *She answered his bow with a curtsy.* **1** *verb,* **2** *noun.*

bread fruit (bred′früt′), a large round fruit that is usually baked or roasted. It grows in very hot climates. *noun.*

bri er (brī′ər), a thorny or prickly plant or bush. The blackberry plant and rosebush are often called briers. *noun.* Also spelled briar.

bril liant (bril′yənt), **1** wonderful, splendid; magnificent: *The singer gave a brilliant performance.* **2** shining brightly; sparkling: *brilliant jewels, brilliant sunshine. adjective.*

bron to sau rus (bron′tə sôr′əs), a large dinosaur of North America that ate plants and lived on land and in the water. *noun.*

bur row (bėr′ō), **1** dig a hole in the ground: *The mole quickly burrowed out of sight.* **2** hole dug in the ground by an animal: *Rabbits live in burrows.* **3** search: *She burrowed in the library for a book about insects.* **1,3** *verb,* **2** *noun.*

C c

camp to sau rus (kamp′tə sôr′əs), a dinosaur that was 4 to 5 feet (1.2 to 1.5 meters) long. It ate plants and walked on either its hind legs or on all four legs. *noun.*

can teen (kan tēn′), **1** a small container for carrying water or other drinks. See picture. **2** a store in a school, camp, or factory where food, drinks, and other articles are sold or given out. *noun.*

cap i tal (kap′ə təl), **1** city where the government of a country or state is located. *Washington, D.C., is the capital of the United States.* **2** A, G, H, K are written here as capital letters. **1** *noun,* **2** *adjective.*

Cap i tol (kap′ə təl), the building in Washington, D.C., in which Congress meets. *noun.*

car di nal (kärd′n əl), a North American songbird. The male has bright-red feathers marked with black. See picture. *noun.*

cardinal—9 inches (23 centimeters) long

cat's-claw (kats′ klô′), a climbing shrub with curved, pointed pods and black, shining seeds. *noun.*

ce dar (sē′dər), an evergreen tree with widely spreading branches. Its fragrant, durable, reddish wood is used for lining clothes closets and for making chests, pencils, and posts. *noun.*

cha me le on (kə mē′lē ən), a small lizard that can change the color of its skin to blend with the surroundings. See picture. *noun.*

canteen (definition 1)

chameleon

chaps (chaps), strong leather riding pants that cowhands wear over their regular pants as protection. *noun.*

Cher o kee (cher′ə kē′), **1** a member of the Iroquois tribe who first came from the southern Allegheny Mountains and who now live mostly in Oklahoma. **2** an Iroquois language. *noun.*

chime (chīm), **1** pieces of wood, metal, or plastic that are hung together, usually in a doorway or outside. When the wind blows through them and they hit each other, they make the sound of musical notes. **2** ring out musically: *The bells chimed at midnight.* **1** *noun,* **2** *verb.*

chord (kôrd), a combination of two or more notes of music sounded at the same time in harmony. *noun.*

clut ter (klut′ər), **1** to litter with things: *The desk was cluttered with papers, strings, and trash.* **2** litter; confusion; disorder: *It was hard to find the lost pen in the clutter of the room.* **1** *verb,* **2** *noun.*

coax (kōks), persuade by soft words; try to convince by being very pleasant and nice: *She coaxed me into letting her use my bike.* *verb.*

co coon (kə kün′), **1** a covering that certain insects spin around their eggs to protect them. **2** silky case spun by caterpillars to live in while they are turning into adult insects: *In the spring a moth came out of the cocoon the caterpillar had spun.* See picture. *noun.*

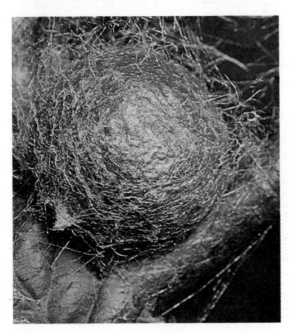

cocoon

a hat	**i** it	**oi** oil	**ch** child	a in about
ā age	**ī** ice	**ou** out	**ng** long	e in taken
ä far	**o** hot	**u** cup	**sh** she	ə = i in pencil
e let	**ō** open	**u̇** put	**th** thin	o in lemon
ē equal	**ô** order	**ü** rule	**ᵺ** then	u in circus
ėr term			**zh** measure	

cog (kog), a wooden or metal tooth on the outer edge of a wooden or metal wheel called a gear. See picture. *noun.*

cog

col lide (kə līd′), crash; hit or strike hard together: *Two ships collided in the harbor and sank.* *verb,* **col lid ed, col lid ing.**

con ti nent (kon′tə nənt), one of the seven great areas of land on the earth. The continents are North America, South America, Europe, Africa, Asia, Australia, and Antarctica. *noun.*

Cor ral Vie jo (kô ral′ vye′hō), a town in Puerto Rico.

cour te sy (kėr′tə sē), a nice way of acting: *Saying thank you to someone who did you a favor is a sign of courtesy. noun, plural* **cour te sies.**

cour ti er (kôr′tē ər), person often present at a royal palace. *noun.*

cre a tion (krē ā′shən), **1** thing that has not been made before: *Sam looked proudly at the machine he had made; it was his creation.* **2** act of making a thing that has not been made before: *The people stood back to watch the artist during her creation of the painting. noun.*

cruis er (krü′zər), **1** a type of car or land machine that is used to search for something. **2** warship with less armor and more speed than a battleship. *noun.*

cur i os i ty (kyu̇r′ē os′ə tē), **1** eager desire to know: *Curiosity got the better of me, and I opened the present two days before I was supposed to.* **2** a strange, rare object: *One of his curiosities was a cane made out of the horn of a deer. noun, plural* **cur i os i ties.**

D d

dag ger (dag/ər), **1** a small knife with a short, pointed blade. **2** a plant that has leaves with sharp points. *noun.*

dain ty (dān/tē), **1** fresh, delicate, and pretty: *The violet is a dainty spring flower.* **2** delicate in tastes and feeling: *A person who is dainty about eating never spills or takes big bites.* **3** good to eat; delicious: *The royal cook prepared many dainty dishes. adjective,* **dain ti er, dain ti est.**

de spair (di sper/ *or* di spar/), **1** loss of hope; being without hope: *We felt despair as the boat started to sink.* **2** person or thing that causes loss of hope: *The students who never did their work were the despair of the teacher.* **3** lose hope; be without hope: *The doctors despaired of saving the patient's life.* **1,2** *noun,* **3** *verb.*

de ter mined (di tèr/mənd), **1** with one's mind firmly made up: *He was determined to go in spite of the storm.* **2** firm; resolute: *Her determined look showed that she had made up her mind. adjective.*

di plod o cus (di plod/ə kəs), a dinosaur that lived in the western part of North America. It was the longest of all the dinosaurs. *noun.*

dis ap point ment (dis/ə point/mənt), **1** the feeling you have when you do not get what you hoped for: *When he did not get a new bicycle, his disappointment was very great.* **2** person or thing that causes disappointment: *The movie was a disappointment to me because it wasn't exciting. noun.*

dis cour age (dis kėr/ij), **1** take away the courage of; destroy the hopes of: *Failing again and again discourages anyone.* **2** try to prevent by disapproving; frown upon: *All her friends discouraged her from such a dangerous swim. verb,* **dis cour aged, dis cour ag ing.**

dis may (dis mā/), **1** sudden loss of courage because of fear or danger; great worry: *They were filled with dismay when they saw the snake.* **2** trouble greatly; make afraid: *The thought that she might fail the test dismayed her.* **1** *noun,* **2** *verb.*

dumb found (dum/found/), completely amaze people so that they can't even say anything: *I was dumbfounded that he could have done such a dreadful thing. verb.*

du o (dü/ō *or* dyü/ō), two people who perform together: *Batman and Robin were called "The Dynamic Duo." noun.*

Ee

ech o (ek/ō), **1** say or do what another person says or does: *As I started talking, I heard the parrot behind me echoing every word I said.* **2** a repeated sound: *You hear an echo when a sound you make bounces back from a distant hill or wall so that you hear it again.* **1** *verb,* **ech oed, ech o ing; 2** *noun, plural* **ech oes.**

el e gant (el/ə gənt), showing good taste; graceful; beautiful: *The palace had elegant furnishings. adjective.*

e mer gen cy (i mėr/jən sē), **1** a sudden need for immediate action: *I keep a box of tools in my car for use in an emergency.* **2** for a time of sudden need: *When the brakes failed, the driver pulled on the emergency brake and stopped the car.* **1** *noun, plural* **e mer gen cies; 2** *adjective.*

em per or (em/pər ər), man who is the ruler of an empire. (An empire is a group of countries.) *noun.*

en gi neer (en/jə nir/), **1** a person who runs the engine of a train; the driver. **2** a person who takes care of or runs engines. **3** a person who is an expert in engineering. **4** guide; manage with skill: *She engineered the whole job from start to finish.* **1,2,3** *noun,* **4** *verb.*

Eng land (ing/glənd), the largest part of the country Great Britain. (Great Britain consists of England, Scotland, Wales, and Northern Ireland.) The people in England speak English. See picture.

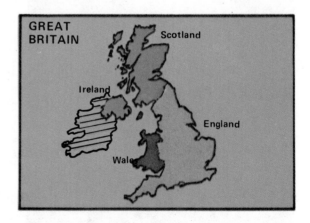

England

368

en ter prise (en′tər prīz), **1** the feeling of being ready to start any big task or project. **2** an important, difficult, or dangerous task or project: *A trip into space is a daring enterprise.* **3** any project: *She has two enterprises—raising hamsters and collecting coins.* noun.

ex haust ed (eg zô′stid), **1** worn out; very tired: *The exhausted hikers stopped to rest after their long walk.* **2** used up: *The babysitter's patience was exhausted by the naughty child.* adjective.

ex hi bi tion (ek′sə bish′ən), **1** a public show: *The art school holds an exhibition of paintings every year.* **2** showing: *I never saw such an exhibition of bad manners before.* noun.

a hat	i it	oi oil	ch child	a in about
ā age	ī ice	ou out	ng long	e in taken
ä far	o hot	u cup	sh she	ə = { i in pencil
e let	ō open	u̇ put	th thin	o in lemon
ē equal	ô order	ü rule	ᴦʜ then	u in circus
ėr term			zh measure	

F f

fal ter (fôl′tər), **1** speak with stops and starts and broken words: *He was so nervous that he faltered when he started talking.* **2** not go straight on; hesitate; waver; lose courage: *I faltered for a moment before making my decision.* verb.

fas ten er (fas′n ər), thing used to tie, lock, or hold together a door or a piece of clothing: *A zipper is a fastener.* noun.

fe ro cious (fə rō′shəs), fierce; savage; very cruel: *I was frightened when I saw the ferocious-looking statue.* adjective.

fetch (fech), **1** go and get; bring: *Please fetch me my glasses.* **2** be sold for: *These eggs will fetch a good price.* verb.

flare (fler *or* flar), **1** a very bright light that burns for a short time, used in time of war or for emergencies on the highway. **2** to flame up briefly, sometimes with smoke: *The wind made the torch flare up.* **3** a sudden burst: *a flare of anger.* **4** spread out in the shape of a bell: *These pants flare at the bottom.* 1,3 *noun,* 2,4 *verb.*

flit (flit), **1** fly lightly and quickly; flutter: *Birds flitted from tree to tree.* **2** pass lightly and quickly: *Many thoughts flitted through my mind as I sat daydreaming.* verb. **flit ted, flit ting.**

freight er (frā′tər), a ship that mainly carries items which will eventually be sold. It does not carry people. *noun.*

fur i ous (fyu̇r′ē əs), **1** full of wild anger: *The owner of the house was furious when she learned of the broken window.* **2** raging; violent: *A hurricane is a furious storm.* adjective.

G g

ga losh es (gə losh′iz), rubbers, worn over the shoes in wet or snowy weather. *noun plural.*

glimpse (glimps), **1** catch a quick look: *I glimpsed the falls as our train went by.* **2** a very short look: *I caught a glimpse of the falls as our train went by.* **1** *verb,* **glimpsed, glimps ing,** **2** *noun.*

gold finch (gōld′finch′), a small yellow songbird marked with black. See picture. *noun, plural* **gold finch es.**

goldfinch

gos sip (gos′ip), **1** talk about other people that is not always true. **2** repeat what one knows or hears about other people. **3** person who gossips a good deal. 1,3 *noun,* 2 *verb.*

gour met (gu̇r′mā), a French word meaning a person who is an expert in judging fine foods. *noun.*

groom (grüm), **1** take care of the appearance of; make neat and tidy. **2** feed, rub down, brush, and generally take care of (horses). **3** person whose work is taking care of horses. **4** bridegroom. 1,2 *verb,* 3,4 *noun.*

H h

herb (ėrb *or* hėrb), **1** plant whose leaves and stems are used for medicine and seasoning. Sage, mint, and lavender are herbs. **2** any flowering plant whose stem lives only one season and does not become woody as the stems of trees and shrubs do. Corn, wheat, lettuce, tulips, and peonies are herbs. *noun.*

hoarse (hôrs), **1** having a rough voice: *A bad cold can make you hoarse.* **2** sounding rough and deep: *the hoarse sound of the bullfrog. adjective,* **hoars er, hoars est.**

hoop skirt (hůp skėrt), a woman's skirt. It stood out from the body because underneath it were bands of metal called hoops that were connected by tapes. *noun.*

hoop skirt

hunch (hunch), **1** bend or form into a hump: *He sat hunched up with his chin on his knees.* **2** a feeling that you don't know the reason for: *I had a hunch it would rain, so I took my umbrella.* **1** *verb,* **2** *noun, plural* **hunch es.**

hur ri cane (hėr′ə kān), storm with violent wind and, usually, very heavy rain. The wind in a hurricane blows at more than 75 miles (120 kilometers) an hour. *noun.*

I i

i mag i nar y (i maj′ə ner′ē), not real: *I used to have dreams during the day and make up imaginary people. adjective.*

im mense ly (i mens′lē), very much; a lot: *We enjoyed the party immensely. adverb.*

im pa tient (im pā′shənt), **1** not willing to accept delay, pain, or bother: *He is impatient with his little brother.* **2** uneasy and eager; restless: *The horses are impatient to start in the race. adjective.*

in dif fer ent (in dif′ər ənt), **1** not caring one way or the other: *I was indifferent to their insults.* **2** unimportant; not mattering much: *We can go whenever you please; the time for starting is indifferent to me.* **3** neither good nor bad; just fair: *an indifferent player. adjective. adverb,* **in dif fer ent ly.**

in ex pen sive (in′ik spen′siv), not costing much money; low-priced. *adjective.*

in no cent (in′ə sənt), **1** doing no harm: *innocent amusements.* **2** doing no wrong or evil; not guilty: *In the United States a person is innocent of a crime until proven guilty.* **3** having and showing the simple and trusting nature of a child. *adjective.*

in quire (in kwīr′), try to find out something by asking questions: *The detective inquired about the lost jewels. verb,* **in quir ed, in quir ing.**

in stinct (in′stingkt), **1** a way of acting that is born in a person or animal without being learned: *Birds do not learn to build nests but build them by instinct.* **2** a natural tendency or ability; talent: *Even as a child, the artist had an instinct for drawing. noun.*

in sult (in sult′ *for 1;* in′sult *for 2*), **1** say or do something rude or harsh to: *She insulted me by calling me a liar.* **2** a rude remark or action: *It is an insult to call someone stupid.* **1** *verb,* **in sult ed, in sult ing.** **2** *noun.*

in tent (in tent′), **1** paying attention; having the eyes or thoughts fixed on something: *A stare is an intent look.* **2** purpose; intention: *I'm sorry I hurt you; that wasn't my intent.* **3** meaning: *What is the intent of that remark?* **1** *adjective,* **2,3** *noun.*

in vis i ble (in viz′ə bəl), cannot be seen: *Thought is invisible. Wind is invisible. adjective.*

i o dine (ī′ə dīn), a medicine put on cuts and bruises to kill germs. *noun*.

I vo ry Coast (ī′və rē kōst), a country in the western part of Africa. See picture.

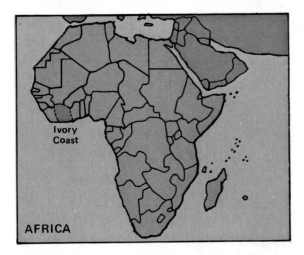

Ivory Coast

a hat	**i** it	**oi** oil	**ch** child	⎧ a in about
ā age	**ī** ice	**ou** out	**ng** long	⎜ e in taken
ä far	**o** hot	**u** cup	**sh** she	ə = ⎨ i in pencil
e let	**ō** open	**ů** put	**th** thin	⎜ o in lemon
ē equal	**ô** order	**ü** rule	**ŦH** then	⎩ u in circus
ėr term			**zh** measure	

L l

la goon (lə gün′), pond or small lake connected with a larger body of water. *noun*.

lei sure ly (lē′zhər lē), without hurry; taking plenty of time: *to stroll leisurely through the park.* *adjective, adverb*.

lens (lenz), the pieces of glass you look through in a pair of eyeglasses. *noun, plural* **lens es.**

leop ard (lep′ərd), a fierce animal in the cat family that is found in Africa and Asia. It has a dull yellowish fur spotted with black. Some leopards are black and may be called panthers. *noun*.

lit ter (lit′ər), **1** young animals born at one time to the same mother: *a litter of puppies.* **2** little bits and scraps left around in an untidy way: *We picked up the litter from the previous day's parade.* **3** scatter things around; leave odds and ends lying around: *You have littered the room with your papers.* See picture. 1,2 *noun*, 3 *verb*.

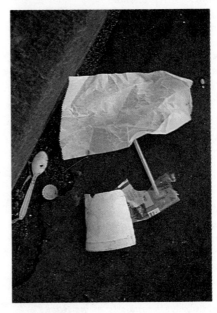

litter (definition 2)

J j

joint (joint), **1** the place in an animal skeleton where two bones join: *The knee or the elbow are joints.* **2** the place at which two things or parts are joined together: *A pocketknife has a joint to hold the blade inside the handle.* **3** one of the parts of which a jointed thing is made up: *the middle joint of a finger.* **4** shared or done by two or more persons: *By our joint efforts we managed to push the car back on the road.* 1,2,3 *noun*, 4 *adjective*.

K k

knap sack (nap′sak′), a leather or canvas bag for clothes or equipment carried on the back. *noun*.

lo cust (lō′kəst), a grasshopper that travels with others in great swarms, destroying the crops. *noun.*

locusts

loom¹ (lüm), machine for weaving cloth. *noun.*

loom² (lüm), appear dimly or vaguely; appear as large or dangerous: *A large iceberg loomed through the thick gray fog. verb.*

lug (lug), pull along or carry with effort; drag: *We lugged the rug to the yard to clean it. verb,* **lugged, lug ging.**

lu mi nous (lü′mə nəs), **1** full of light; bright: *a luminous day.* **2** shining by its own light: *The sun and stars are luminous bodies.* **3** clear; easily understood. *adjective.*

M m

ma gi cian (mə jish′ən), **1** person who entertains by magic tricks. **2** person who can use magic: *The wicked magician cast a spell over the princess. noun.*

maj es ty (maj′ə stē), **1** the title used in speaking to or of a king, queen, or emperor: *Your Majesty, His Majesty, Her Majesty.* **2** stately appearance; royal dignity; nobility: *the majesty of the Rocky Mountains. noun, plural* **maj es ties.**

man go (mang′gō), the slightly sour, juicy fruit of a tree that grows in very hot areas like Puerto Rico. Mangoes are eaten ripe or are pickled for eating when they are green. See picture. *noun, plural* **man goes or man gos.**

mango

math e mat ics (math′ə mat′iks), the science that deals with numbers. Arithmetic is one part of mathematics. *noun.*

mead ow lark (med′ō lärk′), a bird of North America about as big as a robin, having a thick body, short tail, and a yellow breast marked with black. See picture. *noun.*

meadowlark—about 10 inches (25 centimeters) long

me squite (me skēt′), a tree or shrub common in the southwestern United States and Mexico. Mesquite often grows in dense clumps or thickets and bears pods that are used as food for cattle. *noun.*

mis sion (mish/ən), **1** sending or being sent on some special work; errand: *He was sent on a mission to another country.* **2** persons sent out on some special business: *She was one of a mission sent by our government to France. noun.*

moat (mōt), a deep, wide ditch, usually filled with water, dug around a castle or town as a protection against enemies. See picture. *noun.*

moat

mois ture (mois/chər), slight wetness; water or other liquid spread in very small drops in the air or on a surface: *Dew is moisture that collects at night on the grass. noun.*

mon i tor (mon/ə tər), **1** pupil in school with special duties, such as helping to keep order and taking attendance. **2** receiver or other device that is used to check or control something: *Most banks have TV monitors to observe customers and prevent holdups.* **3** check or control something by a receiver or other device: *Police monitor traffic by using cars equipped with radar.* 1,2, *noun,* 3 *verb.*

mo tion (mō/shən), **1** a suggestion made in a meeting, to be voted on: *I made a motion to end the meeting.* **2** movement; moving; change of position or place. Anything is in motion that is not at rest: *Can you feel the motion of the ship? noun.*

mound (mound), **1** a group of things heaped together to form a hill shape: *John poured the nuts out of the big bag until they formed a mound on the table.* **2** bank or heap of earth or stones. **3** the slightly built-up ground from which a baseball pitcher pitches. *noun.*

N n

ña me (nyo/mä), a kind of food that grows in the ground like a potato. It is shaped like a short stick, brown on the outside and white on the inside. *noun, plural* **ña mes.**

a hat	**i** it	**oi** oil	**ch** child		a in about
ā age	**ī** ice	**ou** out	**ng** long		e in taken
ä far	**o** hot	**u** cup	**sh** she	ə =	i in pencil
e let	**ō** open	**ù** put	**th** thin		o in lemon
ē equal	**ô** order	**ü** rule	**ᴛʜ** then		u in circus
ėr term			**zh** measure		

nav i ga tion (nav/ə gā/shən), the science of running or sailing a ship; keeping a ship going in the right direction and knowing where you are at all times. *noun.*

ne ces si ty (nə ses/ə tē), **1** a thing that you can't do without; something that you will need: *Food and water are necessities on a long trip.* **2** something that has to be: *We understand the necessity of eating.* **3** something that forces a person to act in a certain way: *Necessity often drives people to do disagreeable things. noun, plural* **ne ces si ties.**

noc tur nal (nok tėr/nl), **1** active in the night: *The owl is a nocturnal bird.* **2** of the night: *Stars are a nocturnal sight.* **3** in the night: *a nocturnal visitor. adjective.*

noc turne (nok/tėrn/), a musical piece that gives the feeling of night or evening. *noun.*

nurs er y (nėr/sər ē), **1** place or room set apart for the use and care of baby animals or human beings. **2** piece of ground or place where young plants are raised for planting again or sale. *noun, plural* **nurs er ies.**

O o

or nith o mi mus (ôr/nith ō mī/məs), a small dinosaur with no teeth, shaped like a bird. It lived in the western part of North America. *noun.*

out num ber (out num/bər), be more than: *The other team outnumbered us. They had five players and we only had three. verb,* **out num bered, out num ber ing.**

o ver look (ō/vər lùk/), **1** pay no attention to; excuse: *I will overlook the bad things you did this time.* **2** fail to see: *Here are some letters that you overlooked.* **3** have a view from above; be higher than: *This high window overlooks half the city. verb.*

P p

par a sol (par′ə sôl), a light umbrella used to protect oneself from the sun. *noun.*

pat tern (pat′ərn), **1** an arrangement of things in a special way: *Certain stars in the sky form a pattern that looks like a bear.* **2** a guide for something to be made: *The tailor used a paper pattern to make a pair of pants. noun.*

Pe cos (pā′kōs), area around the Pecos River, which flows from northern New Mexico through Texas to the Rio Grande.

per mit (pėr′mit *for 1*; pər mit′ *for 2*), **1** a written order allowing a person to do something: *Do you have a permit to fish in this lake?* **2** let; allow: *My parents will not permit me to stay up late.* **1** *noun,* **2** *verb,* **per mit ted, per mit ting.**

phos pho res cent (fos′fə res′ənt), shining with light; lit up. *adjective.*

plaid (plad), **1** having a pattern of checks or stripes: *a plaid dress.* **2** any cloth with a pattern of checks or crisscross stripes. See picture. **1** *adjective,* **2** *noun.*

plaid (definition 2)

plank ton (plangk′tən), the small animals or plants that float or drift in water, especially at or near the surface. Plankton provides food for many fish. *noun.*

plan ta tion (plan ta′shən), a large farm located in hot climates, where crops like sugar, tobacco, and cotton are usually grown. *noun.*

Pon ce (pun′sā), a city in Puerto Rico.

pool[1] (pül), **1** things or money put together by a group of people to help the whole group: *a car pool.* **2** put (things or money) together for common advantage: *We plan to pool our savings to buy a boat.* **1** *noun,* **2** *verb.*

pool[2] (pül), tank of water to swim or bathe in: *a swimming pool. noun.*

prair ie (prer′ē), a large area of flat land with grass but few or no trees. *noun.*

pre dict (pri dikt′), tell beforehand: *The Weather Service predicts rain for tomorrow. verb.*

pres sure (presh′ər), **1** the continued action of a weight or force: *The pressure from the wind filled the sails of the boat.* **2** a forceful influence: *I was under pressure from the others to change my mind.* **3** force or urge by using pressure: *The car dealer tried to pressure my parents into buying a car.* **1,2** *noun,* **3** *verb,* **pres sured, pres sur ing.**

pre view (prē′vyü′), **1** to see something ahead of the usual time. **2** a look at something ahead of the usual time: *a preview of things to come.* **3** an advance showing of scenes from a play or movie or television program. **1** *verb,* **2,3** *noun.*

priv i lege (priv′ə lij), a special right: *My sister has the privilege of driving the family car. noun.*

pro ces sion (prə sesh′ən), a march; people marching on foot or riding: *We looked out the window to see the royal procession as it passed by.* See picture. *noun.*

procession

proj ect (proj′ekt *for 1,2, and 5;* prə jekt′ *for 3,4*), **1** special job or task. **2** a plan; scheme. **3** put forward on something else: *Movies are projected onto a screen.* **4** stick out: *The rocks project far into the water.* **5** group of buildings built and run together: *a housing project.* 1,2,5 *noun,* 3,4 *verb.*

prong (prông), one of the pointed ends of a fork. *noun. adjective* **pronged.**

pte ran o don (tə ran′ə dən), a flying reptile that lived in North America. It had a wingspan of up to 25 feet (7.5 meters). Its name means "winged-toothless." (It had no teeth.) *noun.*

Puerto Rico (pwer′tō re′kō), island in the eastern part of the West Indies. Many Puerto Ricans live in the United States. See picture.

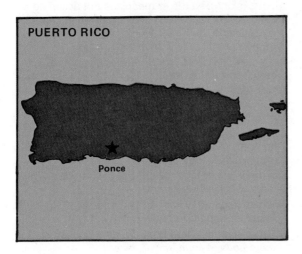

Puerto Rico

pup pe teer (pu pi tēr′), a person who makes puppets perform either by pulling strings that control the puppet's body or, if it is a hand puppet, by moving the hand. *noun.*

R r

ra di ance (rā′dē əns), brightness: *The radiance of the sun. noun.*

a hat	i it	oi oil	ch child	(a in about
ā age	ī ice	ou out	ng long	e in taken
ä far	o hot	u cup	sh she	ə = i in pencil
e let	ō open	ù put	th thin	o in lemon
ē equal	ô order	ü rule	₮H then	u in circus
ėr term			zh measure	

re cess (rē′ses *or* ri ses′ *for 1,3, and 4;* ri ses′ *for 2*), **1** time during which work stops: *Our school has an hour's recess at noon.* **2** take a recess: *The committee recessed for lunch.* **3** part of a wall or other flat surface set back from the rest: *The bench was in the recess of the wall.* **4** an inner place or part: *the recesses of a cave, the recesses of one's secret thoughts.* 1,3,4 *noun,* 2 *verb.*

rel ic (rel′ik), a thing left from the past. See picture. *noun.*

relics

res er va tion (rez′ər vā′shən), **1** land set aside for a special purpose. Many Native Americans live on reservations that the government has set aside for their tribe. **2** a feeling or thought that is kept back: *Joe's mother did not tell him that she had reservations about letting him make the trip alone.* **3** a special way to keep a thing for someone: *Please make my reservation for the hotel room so that when I arrive I'll have a place to stay. noun.*

re signed (ri zīnd′), accepting what happens without complaint. *adjective.*

rick et y (rik′ə tē), weak; shaky; breaking down: *a rickety old chair. adjective.*

ri dic u lous (ri dik′yə ləs), laughable: *It would be ridiculous to walk backward all the time. adjective.*

S s

sched ule (skej′ül), **1** something you make up to arrange the place and time of events and things: *If you look at the train schedule, you will know what times the trains leave during the day.* **2** to arrange things, put them in order: *Let's schedule Mary's songs to be the first on the program.* **1** *noun,* **2** *verb.*

scheme (skēm), **1** plan, plot: *They were scheming to smuggle the stolen jewels into the country.* **2** program of action; plan: *He has a scheme for taking the salt from sea water.* **3** plot: *a scheme to cheat the government.* **1** *verb,* **2,3** *noun.*

scrump tious (skrump′shəs), very pleasing, especially to the taste: *I loved that food. It was scrumptious. adjective.*

sex tant (sek′stənt), a tool that sailors use to find out exactly where they are when they are at sea. With the sextant and the stars and planets in the sky, they can tell how far they are from where they want to go. See picture. *noun.*

sextant

shin gle (shing′gəl), **1** a thin piece of wood, used to cover roofs and walls. **2** cover with such pieces: *shingle a roof.* **1** *noun,* **2** *verb,* **shin gled, shin gling.**

si (sē), Spanish word meaning "yes."

sid ing (sī′ding), **1** a short sidetrack for trains usually connected with the main track by a switch. It is mainly used to allow trains to pass each other to load and unload, and for storing cars that are not being used. **2** the material that forms the sides of a building made of wood. *noun.*

sight (sīt), **1** see: *At last Columbus sighted land.* **2** ability to see: *Birds have better sight than dogs.* **3** range of seeing: *We live in sight of the school.* **4** something that looks bad or odd: *Your room is a sight.* **1** *verb,* **2,3,4** *noun.*

skel e ton (skel′ə tən), **1** bones of a body, fitted together in their natural places. The skeleton is a frame that supports the muscles and organs of the body. **2** frame: *the steel skeleton of a building. noun.*

slang (slang), words or meanings not accepted as standard English when speaking or writing. It is mostly made up of new words or meanings that are popular for only a short time. *noun.*

slay (slā), to kill: *A hunter slays wild animals. verb,* **slew, slain, slay ing.**

soar (sôr), **1** fly at a great height; fly upward: *The eagle soared without flapping its wings.* **2** rise beyond what is ordinary: *Prices are soaring. verb.*

som er sault (sum′ər sôlt), roll or jump, turning the heels over the head. *verb,* **som er sault ed, som er sault ing;** *noun.*

sound¹ (sound), go toward the bottom; dive: *The whale sounded. verb.*

sound² (sound), what can be heard: *the sound of music, the sound of thunder. noun.*

sound³ (sound), free from disease; healthy: *a sound body, a sound mind. adjective.*

spine (spīn), **1** the backbone of a person or animal. **2** a stiff growth on some plants or animals. The thorns of a cactus and the quills of a porcupine are called spines. *noun.*

spoke (spōk), one of the bars from the center of a wheel to the edge (rim) of the wheel. See picture. *noun.*

spoke

squint (skwint), **1** to look with the eyes partly closed: *When Tim took off his glasses, he squinted at the chalkboard to try to make out the words.* **2** a look with the eyes partly closed. 1 *verb*, 2 *noun*.

stalk¹ (stôk), **1** approach or go after without being seen or heard: *The hungry lion stalked a zebra.* **2** spread silently and steadily: *Disease stalked through the land.* **3** walk in a slow, stiff, or proud way: *She stalked into the room and threw herself into a chair.* *verb*, **stalked, stalk ing.**

stalk² (stôk), the main stem of a plant. *noun.*

stam pede (stam pēd′), **1** a sudden scattering or flight of a frightened herd of cattle or horses. **2** any flight of a large group: *the stampede of a frightened crowd from a burning theater.* **3** scatter or flee in a stampede. **4** cause to stampede: *Thunder stampeded the cattle.* 1,2 *noun*, 3,4 *verb*, **stam ped ed, stam ped ing.**

sta tion er y (stā′shə ner′ē), writing materials such as paper, cards, and envelopes. *noun.*

stern¹ (stėrn), the rear part of a ship, boat, or aircraft. *noun.*

stern² (stėrn), severe; strict; harsh: *Our uncle's stern frown silenced us.* *adjective.*

sty ra co sau rus (stī′ra kə sôr′əs), a dinosaur that had a horn on its nose and spikes on the back of its head and neck. It ate plants and moved very slowly. *noun.*

swin dler (swin′dlər), person who cheats others: *That swindler tricked Mike out of all his money!* *noun.*

symp tom (simp′təm), a sign of something: *Fever is a symptom of illness.* *noun.*

Syr i a (sir′ē ə), a country in the western part of Asia. Syrians speak Arabic. See picture.

a hat	**i** it	**oi** oil	**ch** child	a in about
ā age	**ī** ice	**ou** out	**ng** long	e in taken
ä far	**o** hot	**u** cup	**sh** she	ə = { i in pencil
e let	**ō** open	**ù** put	**th** thin	o in lemon
ē equal	**ô** order	**ü** rule	**ŦH** then	u in circus
ėr term			**zh** measure	

T t

tart¹ (tärt), a kind of little cake filled with cooked fruit, jam, or the like. *noun.*

tart² (tärt), **1** having a sharp taste; sour: *Some apples are tart.* **2** sharp: *A tart answer is sometimes not polite.* *adjective.*

tel e scope (tel′ə skōp), an instrument that makes things which are far away seem nearer and larger. You study the stars and planets with a telescope. See picture. *noun.*

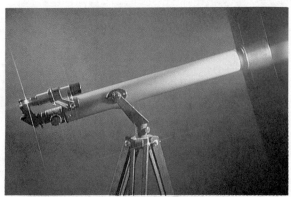

telescope

tem per a ture (tem′pər ə chər), **1** degree of heat or cold. The temperature of freezing water is 32 degrees Fahrenheit or 0 degrees Celsius. **2** a fever; a body temperature higher than normal (98.6 degrees Fahrenheit or 37 degrees Celsius): *A sick person may have a temperature. noun.*

ter ri to ry (ter′ə tôr′ē), **1** land: *Much territory in the northern part of Africa is desert.* **2** land belonging to a government: *Alaska was a territory of the United States until 1958. noun, plural* **ter ri to ries.**

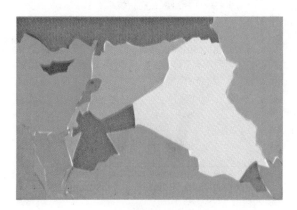

Syria

train (trān), **1** part of a robe, dress, or other piece of clothing that hangs down to the ground. See picture. **2** connected railroad cars moving along together: *A long train traveled down the tracks.* **3** people who follow a leader: *a king and his train.* **4** bring up; teach: *They trained the monkey to do tricks.* 1,2,3 *noun,* 4 *verb.*

train (definition 1)

tread mill (tred′mil′), device for producing a turning motion by having a person or animal walk on the moving steps of a wheel or belt. *noun.*

tri cer a tops (trī sėr′ə tops), a dinosaur that ate only plants. It had three horns, one on its nose and one over each eye. *noun.*

trol ley (trol′ē), a bus that runs on tracks. A pole attached to the roof of the trolley is connected to electric wires. See picture. *noun, plural* **trol leys.**

trolley

trun dle bed (trun′dl bed), a low bed moving on small wheels. *noun.*

tur ret (tėr′it), a small tower, often on the corner of a building. See picture. *noun.*

turrets

twi light (twī′ līt′), the dim light that you see in the sky just before the sun rises and after it sets. *noun.*

ty lo sau rus (tī lə sôr′əs), a sea animal that lived in the time of the dinosaurs, in the midwestern United States around Kansas. It was 20 feet (6 meters) long and looked like a giant lizard. It ate fish. *noun.*

ty ran no sau rus rex (tī ran′ō sôr′əs reks), a dinosaur that ate meat, lived in North America, and walked upright on its two hind legs, like a human being. *noun.*

U u

u ni ty (yü′nə tē), when something is complete or whole with all parts working together perfectly. The many parts of a watch all running together is a perfect example of unity. *noun.*

V v

van ish (van′ish), **1** disappear; disappear suddenly: *The sun vanished behind a cloud.* **2** pass away; cease to be: *Dinosaurs have vanished from the earth.* *verb.*

ven dor (ven′dər), seller: *I saw the ice-cream vendor selling cones on the street.* See picture. *noun.*

vendor

vig or ous (vig′ər əs), strong and active: *The children were vigorous and lively. adjective.*

W w

whip (hwip), **1** beat (cream, eggs, or other foods) to make fluffy and light. **2** strike; beat: *The man whipped the horse to make it go faster.* **3** move, put, or pull quickly and suddenly: *He whipped off his coat.* **4** a thing to strike or beat with: *The lion tamer cracked her whip to get the animals to obey.* **1,2,3** verb, **4** noun.

whirl (hwėrl), **1** move round and round: *whirl a rope.* **2** move or carry quickly: *We were whirled away in an airplane.* **3** a whirling movement: *The dancer suddenly made a whirl.* **4** dizzy or confused way to be: *My thoughts are in a whirl.* **1,2** verb, **3,4** noun.

Y y

yag ua (yo′gwo), the outer covering of a sprouting palm frond. *noun.*

a hat	i it	oi oil	ch child	a in about
ā age	ī ice	ou out	ng long	e in taken
ä far	o hot	u cup	sh she	ə = i in pencil
e let	ō open	ù put	th thin	o in lemon
ē equal	ô order	ü rule	ҬH then	u in circus
ėr term			zh measure	

Z z

za la bi a (za la bē′ə), a thin, crispy wafer from Syria. *noun.*

(Acknowledgments continued from page 2)

"The Queen Who Changed Places with the King" is adapted from "The Queen Who Changed Places with the King" by Nancy West from *Wee Wisdom*, January 1975. © 1974 by Unity School of Christianity. Reprinted by permission of the author.

Reprinted by permission of G. P. Putnam's Sons from PETEY by Tobi Tobias. Copyright © 1978 by Tobi Tobias.

"The Hairy Dog" is reprinted with permission of Macmillan Publishing Co., Inc. and William Heinemann Ltd. from PILLICOCK HILL by Herbert Asquith.

From AN ANTEATER NAMED ARTHUR by Bernard Waber, published by Houghton Mifflin Company. Copyright © 1967 by Bernard Waber. Reprinted by permission.

"What's a Ghost Going to Do?" is adapted from WHAT'S A GHOST GOING TO DO? by Jane Thayer. Copyright © 1966 by Catherine Woolley. By permission of William Morrow & Company.

"My Grandpa and Me" is adapted by permission of Coward, McCann & Geoghegan, Inc. from GRAMPA & ME by Patricia Lee Gauch. Copyright © 1972 by Patricia Lee Gauch.

Adapted from THE SKATES OF UNCLE RICHARD, by Carol Fenner. Copyright © 1978 by Carol Fenner Williams. Reprinted by permission of Random House, Inc.

"Thinking" from AT THE TOP OF MY VOICE AND OTHER POEMS by Felice Holman. Copyright © 1970 by Felice Holman. Used by permission of Charles Scribner's Sons.

"Merlin and Merlin" is adapted from "Merlin and Merlin" by Linda Berry from *Jack and Jill* Magazine. Copyright © 1976 by The Saturday Evening Post Company, Indianapolis, Indiana. Adapted by permission of the publisher.

"The Magic Tube" is adapted from ABRACADABRA! by Barbara Seuling. Copyright © 1975 by Barbara Seuling. Reprinted by permission of Julian Messner, a Simon & Schuster division of Gulf & Western Corporation.

"The Answer-Backer Cure" is an adaptation of "The Answer-Backer Cure" from MRS. PIGGLE-WIGGLE by Betty MacDonald. Text copyright © 1947 by Betty MacDonald. Renewed by Donald C. MacDonald. By permission of J. B. Lippincott, Publishers and Brandt & Brandt Literary Agents, Inc.

"Amos and Boris" adapted from AMOS AND BORIS by William Steig. Copyright © 1971 by William Steig. Reprinted by permission of Farrar, Straus and Giroux, Inc. and Hamish Hamilton, Ltd.

Glossary entries and skill lesson dictionary entries taken or adapted from SCOTT, FORESMAN BEGINNING DICTIONARY. Copyright © 1979, Scott, Foresman and Company, Glenview, Illinois. All Rights Reserved. Also from SCOTT, FORESMAN INTERMEDIATE DICTIONARY. Copyright © 1979, Scott, Foresman and Company, Glenview, Illinois. All Rights Reserved.

ILLUSTRATIONS

Cover: David McCracken
Pages 8–20, Meridith Nemerov; 21, Susan Vaith; 22–24, Morissa Lipstein; 25–36, Bernie Colonna; 37–48, Doug Cushman; 49–51, Morissa Lipstein; 52–58, George Gershinowitz; 62–77, Judith Chang; 78, John Freas; 79–88, Sandy Rabinowitz; 89–92, Morissa Lipstein; 93–102, M. Susan Faiola; 103–124, Claudia Sargeant; 125, John Freas; 126–128, Morissa Lipstein; 130–133, Richard D. Harvey; 134, Map Division, The New York Public Library, Astor, Lenox and Tilden Foundations; 135–139, Richard D. Harvey; 140–151, José Reyes; 152–154, Morissa Lipstein; 155–167, Judith Chang; 168–179, Meridith Nemerov; 182–193, Ralph Pereida; 194–195, Les Morrill; 196–201, Rothberg; 205–207, Morissa Lipstein; 208–220, Pat Milburn; 221–229, Heidi Palmer; 230–242, Dan Siculan; 243, Linda Strauss Edwards; 244–246, Morissa Lipstein; 247–259, Dick Martin; 260–272, Jan Pyk; 273–275, Morissa Lipstein; 276–287, Jennie Williams; 288–303, Allen Davis; 304–305, Nancy Schill; 306–312, Dan Loehle; 313–320, Morissa Lipstein; 321–327, Linda Boehm; 328–333, Linda Miyamoto; 334–346, Irene Trivas; 347–363, William Steig; 364–379, Claudia Sargeant.

PHOTOGRAPHS

Pages 59–60, Yuri Hrynyszyn; 129, Schomburg Center for Research in Black Culture, The New York Public Library, Astor, Lenox and Tilden Foundations; 202, *Photo Researchers, Inc.*; 313, Eric Glenn Johnson; 365, V-DIA/*Editorial Photocolor Archives*; 366 (top right), William T. Shore, *Editorial Photocolor Archives*; 366 (left), Eric Glenn Johnson; 366 (bottom right), V-DIA/*Editorial Photocolor Archives*; 367 (left), V-DIA/*Editorial Photocolor Archives*; 367 (right), Scott, Foresman staff photo; 368, Mel Erikson; 369, V-DIA/*Editorial Photocolor Archives*; 370, *The Bettmann Archive*; 371 (left), Mel Erikson; 371 (right), Eric Glenn Johnson; 372 (left), Gianni Tortoli, *Photo Researchers, Inc.*; 372 (top right), V-DIA/*Editorial Photocolor Archives*; 372 (bottom right), Stephen J. Krasemann, *Photo Researchers, Inc.*; 373, Serraillier, *Photo Researchers, Inc.*; 374 (left), Pagy, *Photo Researchers, Inc.*; 374 (right), *Gamma-Liaison*; 375 (left), Mel Erikson; 375 (right), *Editorial Photocolor Archives*; 376 (left), Lowell Georgia, *Photo Researchers, Inc.*; 376 (right), Laimute Druskis, *Editorial Photocolor Archives*; 377 (left), Mel Erikson; 377 (right), Larry Voight, *Photo Researchers, Inc.*; 378 (top left), Bruce Roberts, *Photo Researchers, Inc.*; 378 (bottom left), Guy Gillette, *Photo Researchers, Inc.*; 378 (right), Tom Hollyman, *Photo Researchers, Inc.*; 379, Tower News Service, *Editorial Photocolor Archives*.

STUDIO

Educational Graphics, Inc.